LIVING IN THE SPIRIT OF LOVE

Heart
of God

BY SISTER VALENTIA LEIBEL, SSND

LIVING IN THE SPIRIT OF LOVE

Heart of God

BY SISTER VALENTIA LEIBEL, SSND

© 2014 by Valentia Leibel

Cover & book layout & design and illustration: Doowah Design Inc.
Original artwork inspiration for cover design: Sister Gemma Golina
Author photo: Alex Semenoff of TRIO Imagery
Editor: Suzanne Paschall

Produced by Indie Ink Publishing's Story Incorporated
#220, 220 20th Street West
Saskatoon, SK, Canada S7M 0W9
T 888.438.1343

Printed in Canada by Friesens, Inc.
First edition: April, 2014
ISBN 978-1-927714-05-8

Also available in e-book form
978-1-927714-06-5

Library and Archives Canada Cataloguing in Publication
Leibel, Valentia
[Essays. Selections]
      Heart of God : living in the spirit of love / by Sister
Valentia Leibel, SSND.
ISBN 978-1-927714-05-8 (pbk.)
      1. Christian life—Catholic authors. I. Title.
BX2350.3.L45 2014   248.4'82   C2014-900670-5

MIX
Paper from
responsible sources
FSC   FSC® C016245
www.fsc.org

CONTENTS

FOREWORD

Heart of God: Living in the Spirit of Love, is a collection of wisdom and knowledge gleaned from the author's commitment to serve as a member of the School Sisters of Notre Dame. Sister Valentia Leibel has dedicated her life to bring the message of God's unconditional love to those she serves. She cares deeply about relationships that shape peoples' lives.

Heart of God takes us on a reflective journey based on personal experiences with people around the world. It gives us an intimate glimpse at Sister Val's relationship with God and all creation, and challenges us to examine and better understand our own relationships. This book celebrates the goodness of people and recognizes our need to accept and forgive. The simple yet profound language used to tell the stories is engaging and delightful.

Heart of God has a detailed table of contents which enables you, the reader, to pick and choose the "bits and bites" you wish to use as food for your soul, according to your present need or interest.

Sister Val has the capacity to listen openly, without judgment, and hears with her heart. She has served in many capacities in the ministries to which she was called—teacher, catechist, parish worker, pastoral minister and ministering to the aged and others. Like our foundress, Blessed Theresa, Sister Val lives out of the conviction that "the world can be changed through the transformation of persons." (SSND CONSTITUTION)

Enjoy the bountiful fruits of this labour of love.

Catherine C. Reschny, B.ED (retired)
Author's sister

Sister Kathleen Cornell, SSND, Ph.D.
Provincial Leader
School Sisters of Notre Dame
Atlantic-Midwest Province

PART ONE:
WHO IS GOD?

The trillium petals are a symbol of the Blessed Trinity, sharing in the divine love which is centred in the heart of God. From the centre of that immense heart, God's grace emanates as an abundant gift to us all. This is symbolized in the concentric circles of divine wisdom and love permeating all of creation, altering our experience, energizing our emotions, leading to conversion of heart and eventually to the oneness for which Jesus prayed.

The spreading seed depicts the extravagant, compassionate hope in a future of love and justice, a harmony and peace that is a glimpse of the reign of God in our midst.

Original Illustration: Sister Gemma Golina, SSND.

GOD

There probably is no God, so enjoy your life.

I was intrigued by this advertisement on the side of city buses. 'Probably' tells us that the authors are not sure that there is no God, or that there is. They also assume that if there is a God, life may not be enjoyed. I would like to know what kind of a God these folks don't believe in.

As a catechist and pastoral worker, I encountered some interesting images of God people have. A teenager claimed he had to be an atheist since he just couldn't believe in the God he envisioned. "What is this God like?" I asked. "He is an old man with a long beard just waiting to catch me doing something wrong so he can punish me." Well, I don't believe in that God either. Human language is so limited in trying to describe who God is and always falls short. A woman in her 80s returning from Bible study said with anger and tears: "Why do we call God our Father? My father was the meanest man who ever lived. I cannot imagine a God who is a father."

Catechist
A teacher of religion.

The parents of a teenaged son who committed suicide visited me to ask, "Where is our son now? He took his own life and he didn't believe in God." When they found him he was still alive and his mother rode in the ambulance with him. He kept saying, "Mom, I'm sorry; I love you." Did he have true love in his heart? The love we have to share is a gift from God who is LOVE. If this boy would have known God as Love, he would have been a believer. Surely, God, who is LOVE, would welcome him home.

On their first day in junior high, four boys approached me in religion class to tell me they were atheists. I asked them if they had ever believed. Of course they had, when they made their First Communion, when they were altar servers. I suggested that the faith they had then was faith based on the faith of their parents, teacher and priest. They were struggling to believe on their own. "Now, if you ever come to believe again, it will be your very own faith." At the end of class one of these 'atheists' offered this prayer, "Dear God, help us to know who you really are!"

Years ago I studied philosophy of religion. The professor, who claimed to be an atheist, said that it is impossible to scientifically prove the existence of God since all proofs, including Thomas Aquinas', begin with the premise that there is a God. When asked, he conceded that he couldn't scientifically prove the existence of love either.

We get into trouble when we try to pin God down, as it were, with the best description. Scripture has numerous ways of describing God, all of them inadequate, because God is pure Spirit—unfathomable mystery. Jesus called God his Father and taught us to do so. He also said, "To have seen me is to have seen the Father." (JOHN 14:9) In the gospels we see Jesus dining with sinners, hugging children, forgiving, healing, teaching, bringing Good News to all. Jesus is described as shepherd, a woman searching for a lost coin, a mother hen, the Light of the World, the Way, the Truth and the Life, to list but a few metaphors.

Whenever we restrict our idea of God to one or two images, we make God restricted too, so that our own minds can understand and describe in full. That is great pride indeed. Let us remember, "...everyone who loves is born of God and knows God...for God is love."

> *God of Love*
> *Help us to realize you are with us always*
> *Amen*

MADE IN THE IMAGE OF GOD

God created humankind in his image, in the image of God he created them; male and female he created them. (GENESIS 1:27)

A little girl was asked what she was drawing. "I'm drawing God," she said proudly. "But no one knows what God looks like," she was told. "They will when my picture is finished!"

How did God in her picture look? Perhaps he resembled her mom or dad or some other person important to her. And she would have been quite right. I see images of God every day: a young father holding his infant son or daughter; a mom preparing a meal to feed her hungry family; an adult and a couple of young people delivering Meals on Wheels; Someone delivering groceries to the elderly; courtesy car drivers; teachers being patient with active children. The list is as long as we can think of people doing what is God-like.

God is LOVE. Every thought, word and action done in love is image of God. God is *forgiving*. Every act of forgiveness we bestow on others or ourselves is imaging God. God is *just*. Every effort to bring justice to the oppressed, the marginalized, the poor, or to make our world a more just society is imaging the just God. God is *creative*. Parents giving birth and creating family are the image of God. Artists who create music, poetry, sculpture and paintings are imaging God, who is always creating. We all have the grace to become an ever better image of God, "because God's love has been poured into our hearts through the Holy Spirit that has been given to us." (ROMANS 5:5)

The human person who is the perfect image of God is Jesus Christ, also being God. We can learn from him how to improve our imaging of God by doing what he did and does; by following his example. Jesus said to Philip who wanted to see God, "Lord, show us the Father and we will be satisfied." Jesus replied, "Whoever has seen me has seen the Father." (JOHN 14:8-9) If we keep our eyes on Jesus, reading the gospels for inspiration, we will certainly become ever better at imaging God. And just as Jesus says, "To see me is to see the Father," could we not be able to say, "To see me is to see Jesus"?

Have you seen Jesus lately? Have you seen God? There is an account of a little barefoot boy looking into the window of a shoe store. It was December. A woman asked what he was doing to which he responded, "I am asking God to give me shoes." The woman took him into the store bought him six pairs of socks, washed his feet and clothed them with socks and shoes. As she was leaving him he asked her, "Are you God's wife?" Since God has no gender she was truly God to this little boy. Children have a way of recognizing goodness and attributing it to God. May we become as little children for to them the kingdom of heaven belongs.

Dear God

As we meet one another

may we be aware that we are meeting special people

made in your image and likeness

Thank you for showing us your face in all the people we meet

Amen

THE GIFT OF LOVE

Valentine's Day seems to be the time of year when conventional wisdom expects that people will express their love for one another. From early January, businesses begin displaying valentine candy, valentine cards and all kinds of valentine trinkets.

Love is one of the most misused and abused words in the English language. The dictionary defines love this way: "to have great affection, feel sexual passion for, enjoy something very much, a beloved person, score of nothing in tennis and squash." We love chocolate, hockey, earrings, a sweater; we love to skate, to read, to listen to music; we love our job, our car, our pets. And we love our spouse and children, our friends and neighbours. And most of all we love God.

Are all the above uses of the word equal in meaning? Of course not. In our faith, in our spiritual life love is holy, gift of God who is love. "Whoever does not love does not know God, for God is love." (1 JOHN 4:8) If we know how to love it is because God's love is within us. "In this is love, not that we loved God, but that God loved us." (1 JOHN 4:10) In verse 12, "If we love one another God lives in us, and God's love is perfected in us." This is the love that is called *agape*, the love that extends to all people.

What does this mean in our daily lives? God loves each one of us unconditionally. There is nothing you or I can do to get God to not love us. God is love. That is what God does. Because God loves us we are also forgiven. In LUKE 7:36 FF, there is the story of a woman, a known sinner, who was forgiven and therefore was able to love. Jesus says, "Therefore her sins, which were many, have been forgiven; hence she has shown great love." Do I really and truly believe in the depths of my heart that I am so loved by the God who made me, the God of the universe, the God of all ages? Can it be that this great God chooses to live in me and gift me with the same love with which all creation is loved? Am I really precious in God's eyes, and honoured and loved? (ISAIAH 43:4)

> *God of Love*
> *I believe that every person is created in your image*
> *and loved unconditionally by you*
> *Yes, even the one who has recently humiliated me, the one who gossips*
> *about me*
> *the one who does not like me, even the one I don't like*
> *Jesus challenges us to "Love one another as I have loved you"*
> *May our families and communities also believe in your unconditional*
> *and very personal love for them*
> *May we work together to change our world so that all will know that you*
> *are a God of Love*
> *Amen*

IS IT FAIR?

A landowner hired laborers to work in his vineyard. At the end of the day all received a day's wage, the amount agreed upon for those who labored 12 hours. It was what was needed to live on for a day. Those that worked only one hour had the same needs so the generous owner gave them what they needed not what they earned. The kingdom of heaven is like this. (Matthew 20:1-16)

The workers who put in a 12 hour day of hard labor cried, "Unfair!" Had the others not received as much they would have been satisfied. God's ways are not our ways. People who are faithful all their lives from baptism on receive the grace they need. Sinners, lately converted also receive whatever grace they need. All are treated equally. In God's reign there are no haves and have-nots. Everyone has all they need.

We are called to be like God who lets the rain fall and the sun shine on the just and unjust alike. If we as society were a little more like God, there wouldn't be a growing gap between the rich and poor. Everyone would share in the abundance that our Creator lavishly provides through Mother Earth. No one would starve while others hoard more, much more, than they need. Is it fair that we need food banks, that minimum wage is not a living wage, that while people starve others keep growing richer? Is it fair?

A man had two sons. The younger couldn't wait for his father to die to receive his inheritance, so he asked and received it right away. We know what he did with it. When he found himself starving while servants in his father's employ had plenty, he decided to ask his father to hire him as a servant. Instead, he was given a royal welcome with a great party and given back his status as son. (Luke 15:11-32)

The elder brother who had been faithful all along cried, "Unfair!" Not only did his younger brother squander half of their father's property, he is taken back and given another chance at being son and heir. Is it fair?

Truly God's ways are not our ways. God's sense of fairness differs greatly from ours. No matter how many times we sin and wander away from our God, we are always welcomed back with open arms and invited to share in the life of God's family.

We are called to be like God, ready to forgive, to give yet another chance to anyone who has sinned against us. And we are invited to return to faithfulness as often as we wander, assured of being received, forgiven and celebrated. *This* is fair, to treat others as we are treated by God.

With these two parables Jesus teaches us that God's generosity knows no bounds, that God's unconditional love levels the field for all, sinner and saint alike, that God has no favourites. And Jesus calls us to be more like God, generous, fair to all, forgiving and grateful. *Is this fair?*

> *Loving God*
> *Give us the courage to do as you do*
> *Treating everyone according to need*
> *May we be generous to all*
> *Amen*

MOTHERS – IMAGE OF GOD

Every year we honour our mothers on a May Sunday we call Mother's Day. Mothers are celebrated with breakfast in bed, flowers, chocolates, family gatherings and other creative ways. As I reflect on mothers— my own mother, the many mothers in my life, I am struck by how like God they are.

Mothers give birth, nurse their infants and bathe, feed and clothe them into adulthood. Mothers teach, admonish, forgive, kiss hurts away, love unconditionally and always.

Mother's work is never done. She is available 24/7 to the needs of her family.

God has many motherly attributes we recognize in our own mother.

> There is in God such a plenitude of life that Israel gives God the names of father and mother. To express the merciful tenderness of God, *rahamim* (compassion) denotes the maternal sentiments and evokes an interior emotion that a woman feels for her children. (PSALMS 25:6 and 116:5) God consoles us as a mother, (ISAIAH 66:13) and if one could be found to forget the child of her womb, God will never forget. (ISAIAH 49:15)
>
> Wisdom, which is the Word of God, relates to God's children as a mother, teaching them, nourishing them with bread, giving them water to drink. (Sir 15:2ff)
>
> (FROM *Dictionary of Biblical Theology*, XAVIER LEON-DUFOUR)

God gives birth, nurtures us, admonishes us, feeds us in Eucharist, Holy Communion, forgives us, loves us unconditionally and forever. God's work never finishes. Jesus tells us, "My Father is still working, and I also am working." God is available to us, with us, 24/7.

Pope John Paul I said memorably that just as God is truly our Father, even more is God our Mother, especially when we are in trouble through sin.

So mothers, we salute you, we honour you. We look to you when we need to know the compassionate love of God. We are grateful that you gave us birth and have raised us to know and love God whom you image so well. You love us even when we are wayward. Your love and caring follows us in all our travels, all our activities, all the ups and downs in our lives. May every day be Mothers' Day in our minds and hearts. And so we offer this prayer of blessing:

> *May God wrap her warmth around you*
> *Like a shawl to hug you tight*
> *May God's light glow bright within you*
> *To guide your steps at night*
> *May God's strength flow sure all through you*
> *Hold you up against hurt and fear*
> *May God whisper in your heart*
> *"Mother, my love is always near"*
> *Amen*
>
> (BY EDWINA GATELEY)

DO YOU KNOW...?

A human body can bear only up to 45 del (unit of pain)
But at the time of giving birth,
A woman feels up to 57 del (unit) of pain.
This is similar to 20 bones getting fractured at a time.
Love our mother,
The most beautiful person on this earth,
Our best critic, yet our strongest supporter.

FATHERS – IMAGE OF GOD

Every year we honour our fathers on a June Sunday we call Fathers' Day. It is a day on which we celebrate our fathers to show them our love and thanks. Fathers remind us of God in so many ways.

Fathers are strong, protecting, providing for our needs, loving us no matter what. They encourage us to be our best, challenge us to greater efforts and support us in our dreams. Fathers love our mothers as Christ loves the Church, teaching us about relationships by example. When we first learn to pray the 'Our Father' the image we have is that of our own dad.

Jesus is the perfect image of the Father: "To have seen me, is to have seen the Father." (JOHN 14:9) We perceive and learn through our senses. Jesus used this by telling "picture stories" about God. So when we read stories like the Good Shepherd and the Prodigal Son, do we not see how fathers love like that, unconditionally and forgiving, always ready to welcome us home?

The very best way fathers are image of God is to be of the same mind and heart as Jesus Christ. He is the perfect image of the Father. Being like him is to be a good image of God.

So fathers, we salute you and honour you. We look to you when we need to know the protecting, welcoming, unconditional love of God. We thank you for being there for us, for sharing our dreams and encouraging our efforts. On Fathers' Day you will be celebrated in special family ways. But you are special every day, even when we forget to let you know.

We pray a blessing on you

The Lord bless you and keep you

The Lord make his face shine upon you

The Lord lift up his countenance upon you

And be gracious to you

And give you peace

Amen

(NUMBERS 6:14-26)

THE MANY FACES OF GOD

PSALM 105:4 asks us to "seek God's presence continually." It is a challenge to be continually aware that we are always in God's presence and that God is always present with us. Life itself teaches us with all our interactions with other people and nature. Everywhere I look, everywhere I am, I see, hear and feel God's loving presence.

When I am out walking I often meet a mom or dad with a baby in arms or stroller and one or two toddlers on bike or tricycle enjoying the fresh air and sunshine. The innocent faces of the children remind me of what Jesus said about them: "Let the little children come to me, for it is to such as these that the Kingdom of God belongs." (MARK 10:14) I see the face of Jesus in the children I meet, and in the mom and or dad, the image of God as mother and father of us all. Thanks to all the moms and dads and their little ones for showing me such a beautiful face of God. When I see them I am very aware that I am in God's presence.

At other times I meet children coming from school or a sporting event. They are chatting with one another, riding bikes and at times so exuberant because "we just came back from Table Mountain! It was so great!" These young people with their energy and love of life show me another face of Jesus who looks on them with love and pride. And if I would meet their teachers, I would see the face of Jesus, the Teacher.

I see elderly people out with their walkers and canes still living life as fully as possible. Here in Heritage Manor we are all seniors. If you could hear the conversations, the teasing and laughter that ring out the joy of being together for bingo, a supper or other activity, you would know that God is indeed present among us.

Teachers occasionally bring their class to learn with us. For example, we have done math bingo with grade four and had grade two children read to us. These intergenerational gatherings are ways of being family of God.

There are so many other people: pastors, service people in local businesses, health care personnel, all show some facet of God's unconditional caring love among us.

Nature speaks especially loudly of God's presence: the birds chirping, the wind playing in the trees and flapping flags, to name a few sounds. Seeing the branches waving reminds me of what sounded "like a powerful wind from heaven" on the day of Pentecost. (ACTS 2:2) Wind and rain always remind me of the presence of the Holy Spirit who came to each of us at our baptism and confirmation.

"Seek God's presence continually." Perhaps it isn't as challenging as it seems at first. It asks of us to be aware and open, to stop occasionally from our hectic schedules to be aware of the sights and sounds around us.

We are signs of God's presence among us!

AMBASSADORS OF GOD

Climate change, global warming, is a scientific problem, and a political issue. It is also a faith matter. Every time we listen to the news or read a paper, this issue is brought to our attention. Science makes predictions of dire consequences if we do not immediately change our ways. Political rhetoric seems to be for political gain. But our Christian faith response must be one of hope.

In the beginning God created the heavens and the earth. When all was completed culminating in humankind made in the image and likeness of God, God saw everything he had made, and indeed, it was very good. God blessed us saying, "Be fruitful and multiply and fill the Earth and subdue it." According to The Jerome Biblical Commentary, this was not a license to exploit the Earth. Rather it was the commission to be God's ambassadors. Eerdmans Commentary is also helpful in this regard: "...every human being, male and female, is God's representative who governs the rest of creation on God's behalf. This is not a mandate to exploit the earth but to manage the earth for the benefit of all creation...God is always portrayed as solicitous for the welfare of his creation; so obviously (we) should be too."

Certainly much of what we have done and do to our Earth does not benefit all creation. Earth Day is a time for us to examine our collective conscience regarding our care of the Earth. How can we become better managers, better ambassadors for God whose creation it is? Like with many of our mistakes, is it possible to put the past behind us and start over? Where can we find hope? We know that the whole creation has been groaning in labour pains until now; and not only creation, but we ourselves who have the first fruits of the Spirit groan inwardly... (ROMANS 8:22-23)

God is still creating: See, I am making all things new. (REVELATION 21:5) And God still sees all creation as very good. And God is still blessing us, asking us to manage the earth for the benefit of all creation in God's name. We are still privileged to be God's ambassadors. How do we do this? It takes a change in attitude which leads to finding creative ways to change our behaviour. Each of us, as an Ambassador of God, is challenged to find ways to care for the welfare of all of God's creation. The Earth is the Lord's and all that is in it, the world, and those who live in it. (PSALM 24:1)

We have the first fruits of the Spirit, and this gives us wisdom, understanding and courage to know and do what we need to do.

> *Hear us, Creator God*
> *and be with us every day*
> *as we seek to restore and preserve your creation*
> *Amen*
>
> (FROM THE CENTER OF CONCERN, EDUCATION FOR JUSTICE)

LOOK ON GOD AND BE RADIANT

"Look to God that you may be radiant with joy, and your faces may not blush with shame." (Psalm 34:6)

These days we may have many reasons to look sad and ask God, "Why? Why all the natural disasters? Why so much anger, hatred, unrest and violence? Why are there leaders who are so power-hungry that they stop at nothing, even killing their own people to hang on to that power? How can we look to you, God, and not have sad, confused and maybe even angry faces? Can we look to *you* and be radiant with joy and our faces will not be ashamed? This doesn't seem possible. And yet, with you all is possible.

On the second Sunday of Lent we contemplated on the Transfiguration of Jesus described in Matthew 17:2. "He was transfigured before them, and his face shone like the sun, and his clothes became dazzling white." When God's voice from a bright cloud spoke, "This is my Son, the Beloved; with him I am well pleased; listen to him," the disciples fell to the ground in fear. But Jesus touched them. When they looked up they saw only Jesus.

Can we look up and see only Jesus, even in these dire times? Our faith tells us that all that God created belongs to God, is loved by God. Even in the chaos, God is there and God's face can be seen in all the good that is also happening: people in Japan helping one another in searching for missing loved ones, in burying loved ones and grieving with those left behind. In Libya, too, there surely are many ways that God shows his face if we only know how and where to look. The same is true of all the other suffering, struggling, warring nations. It is also true right in our midst. Let us look up and see only Jesus.

The mother of a little girl walking home from school during a thunderstorm was worried that she would be very frightened and so drove to meet her. To her surprise, the child was walking along slowly, stopping every few steps, looking up at the sky with a big smile. What was she doing? She explained, "God is taking my picture so I give him a big smile." Children know how to look to God with a smile.

Back to verse 6 of Psalm 34: "Look to God that you may be radiant with joy, and your faces may not blush with shame." Our Lenten practices also need shining and smiling faces. "Whenever you fast, do not look dismal...When you fast put oil on your head and wash your face." (Matthew 6:16-17) Perhaps we will be seeing many radiant faces, looking on God and not blushing with shame. Then we can pray: (Psalm 34:1-4)

I will bless the Lord at all times
God's praise shall continually be in my mouth
My soul makes its boast in the Lord
Let the humble hear and be glad
O magnify the Lord with me, and let us exalt God's name together
Amen

JESUS IN DISGUISE

A certain woman worked among the homeless, the addicts, the down-and-outers, the least among God's children. After a late night shift she boarded the bus for home. There was just one other passenger. He was dirty, smelly and very drunk. Her response? "Jesus, this is your best disguise ever." This gave me the title for this article. What are some of Jesus' other disguises?

Jesus said, "I am with you always, to the end of the age." (Matthew 28:20) Have you seen him? Where is he? How is Jesus with us?

A group of salesmen, in a hurry to catch their flight, accidentally knocked over a table which held a display of apples for sale. One of them chose to miss his flight to help the blind girl pick up her apples. He helped her to arrange her display and paid generously for those that were bruised. As he walked away to see about another flight she called after him. "Mister, are you Jesus?" Was he Jesus for her? Are you sometimes mistaken for Jesus?

On a cold December day a little boy, barefoot and shivering with cold, was standing by a shoe store peering through the windows. A lady approached and said, "My, you are in deep thought." "I was asking God to give me a pair of shoes." The lady took him into the store, asked the clerk to get him six pairs of socks. Then she took him to the back of the store with a basin of water and a towel. She knelt down, washed and dried his feet, put on a pair of socks and bought him a pair of shoes. As she turned to go, the astonished youngster asked, "Are you God's wife?" What a disguise this was! This story calls to mind how Jesus washed the feet of his disciples. He told them, "I have set you an example that you also should do as I have done to you." (John 13:15)

We are the presence of Jesus whenever we act like he would. He says he is the light of the world (John 8:12) He also says to us, "You are the light of the world....Let your light shine before others..." (Matthew 5:14-15) Whenever we act as Jesus would, we are the way Jesus is with us till the end of the age.

There is another kind of presence that Jesus asks us to recognize. "Whatever you do to the least, you do to me." (Matthew 25:40) In the examples above, the blind girl was Jesus to the salesman; and the barefoot boy was for the lady who helped him. What about the dirty, smelly, drunk passenger on the bus. The woman who shared the bus with him could have been afraid, but she saw one of the least that Jesus speaks about in Matthew's last judgment scene.

Each of us is challenged to be Jesus' presence for others. I am sometimes the helping, foot-washing Jesus and sometimes I am the needy Jesus who needs another's ministry.

Have you seen Jesus in disguise lately? How have you been Jesus in disguise?

> Lord Jesus
>
> Your are among us in many disguises
>
> May we not be so blind as to overlook
>
> your presence
>
> however you choose to be
>
> Amen

PART TWO:
QUEST FOR GOD: OUR HUMAN CONDITION

BEING HUMAN

November is the time when we remember our loved deceased ones. November 1, All Saints Day; November 2, All Souls Day; and November 11, Remembrance Day, for all who died in wars. Each year more loved ones and more soldiers are added to our list to remember and pray for. Who will be next? It gives us cause to reflect on the reality of our mortality, what it means to be human. My reflection is based on an experience during a retreat years ago in a wooded area of northern Ontario.

I walked through the woods luxurious in growth. As I kicked through the thick carpet of leaves I noticed that all that growth comes out of dead things. The leaves are dead, forming the rich humus as they rot to provide nourishment for new and renewing life. Fallen trees are dead, yet alive with lichens, fungi, and sometimes new shoots of their own kind. Beneath my feet the very earth was pulsating with life. I stood in the stillness and listened to the dying and the living: the quiet flutter of falling leaves, the crackling of dead wood; the almost imperceptible sounds of insect life all around, the birds, the music of the breezes playing the treetops. I looked up at the towering trees deeply rooted in the earth and reaching for the heavens. I stood in awe and wonder feeling my littleness and rejoicing at the greatness of my being. I felt humble and little in God's presence. I note and reflect on the similarity of the words humus, human and humble.

Humanness is everything that is shared by all of us who are fashioned, male and female, in the image and likeness of our Creator God. I have no humanity except that which I share with every man, woman and child, past, present and future. It is OUR humanity. And we have no humanity but that which has something in common with "humus," the soil from which we were taken, as well as with our Creator God who fashioned us to be like himself. "Yahweh God fashioned man of dust from the soil."(GENESIS 2:7) "God created him, male and female he created them." (GENESIS 1:27)

As "humus" we die, decay, give ourselves for nourishment of life. As image of God we stretch beyond ourselves to the very life of God, eternal *love*. The humanity we are called to accept is both limited and dying and limitless into eternal life. We can no more accept the one aspect without the other than we can pick up the outside of a cup without its inside.

How do we go about accepting our humanity? What is this act of acceptance? To accept is to receive, as is, without desiring to change what is given. The gift of our humanity implies letting God be God, the Giver of all that is, and being content with me being me, the one gifted by God. Acceptance is taking God's word of covenant to heart, "I will be your God, and you will be my people." (JEREMIAH 30:22) It is living out of that reality, letting God be in charge, taking our creaturely role.

Acceptance is different from passivity. To accept is not just to receive passively. To accept means to be responsible for what I accept. If I accept a charges-reversed phone call, I am responsible for the cost. We accept and are responsible for *our* humanity. Responsibility implies caring for, nurturing, making whole, healing, forgiving, giving, freeing. It also implies being cared for, being nurtured, being made whole, being healed, being forgiven, being given to, being made free. Mutuality stems from this humanity being OURS. Accepting our humanity means being in union with all others, or at least striving to be.

For us Christians, the central reality of our humanity is that it is shared by Jesus Christ. So to accept our humanity means to be "of the same mind as Christ Jesus. His state was divine yet he did not cling to his equality with God but emptied himself...and became as humans are...he was humbler yet." (PHILIPPIANS 2:5-9) We have no humanity save that which Jesus Christ shares with us. The mutuality of our acceptance of our humanity includes mutuality with Jesus, the "first born of all creation," the head of the body, the church. Through him, in union with him, we live the very life of God.

With such lofty thoughts, where is our humility? Humility is truth. To be humble is to be true, to be who we really are, humus, human, and children of God. "Think of the love that the Father has lavished on us by letting us be called God's children; and that is what we are." (1 JOHN 3: 1-2) Yes these are lofty thoughts, God's thoughts which are as high above ours as the heavens are above the earth. We accept what is given without desiring to change it. We are God's gift. That is the truth of humbly being human.

Thank you, Lord Jesus, for sharing our humanity

so that we are privileged to share your inheritance as children of God

Amen

FINDING OUR ROOTS

Why do so many former citizens of a town return for a milestone, like a 100th anniversary?

Why do adopted children frequently search for their birth mother, father?

Why do people who are introduced to me ask to which Leibel family I belong?

These and other questions gave me cause to reflect on the importance of knowing our roots. Family roots are crucial to knowing who we are. It is our family ancestry that gives us our genes, our looks, our character makeup. This is why adopted children feel the need to find their family of origin. Abandoned children, victims of war, are often given a name, an identity different from their own because it is unknown by authorities. They may never know who they really are. And their offspring will know only that their ancestor was an unknown refugee.

The community in which we grow up, the schools we attend, the church that nourishes our faith and helps to establish our identity as God's children, all these also help us grow into the people we have become, are becoming. That is why people return to their home town, why family reunions take place, why history books of local areas are produced.

Each local community has its own character and its residents are often defined by it. This happened to Jesus. "Can anything good come from Nazareth?" (JOHN 1:46) While where we come from is very important to who we are, it is only the beginning. We are personally responsible for how we develop, for our priorities, our decisions. It wasn't fair to judge Jesus by his hometown. In fact it wasn't fair to judge Nazareth negatively. It is never right to judge people by their ethnic backgrounds, their families of origins, or their environments. We have each been given the raw materials of our life and personhood. These are great gifts with which to become the person God has intended us to be. And it is a lifetime task.

So why do so many people return to celebrate a community's 100th anniversary? Could it be that instinctively we need to connect again and again with our origins, meet again the people who have influenced our lives, renew our self-knowledge? My community, called "Unity" recently did just that. Together we are the people of Unity (pun intended), in the province of Saskatchewan. Canada is our country, Earth our home planet within the solar system in the Milky Way galaxy within the Virgo supercluster of galaxies, in the universe, all created by a loving God.

We cannot know truly who we are until we acknowledge our interconnectedness with all that is. As Christian people, baptized into the Body of Christ, our roots go back to Jesus Christ and, in him, to the Creator God who knew us from the dawn of creation.

Let us live our heritage well!

Amen

BEING FULLY ALIVE

Jesus gives as his reason for coming into our world, "that we may have life – life in all its fullness." (JOHN 10:10) St. Irenaeus, a 4th century martyr, said that "the glory of God is the human being fully alive." What does it mean to be fully alive? What are the signs?

It is said that it takes a lifetime to become who we are. So it must also take time to become fully alive, one day at a time.

Nature springs to life in spring and flowers to fullness in summer and fall. Summer also brings people outdoors to garden, work fields, play, enjoy the sunshine and cottages. It seems that people are more alive in summer than in winter. Yet the winter sleep of nature is vital for the growth of spring and summer.

The winters in our lives are also vital for our spiritual growth. When sickness disables us for a short or long while we can still live life to the full by the kind of attitude we have. Is it one of self-pity or do we decide to make the most of it and remain positive and grateful? When everything that could, does go wrong in family, work, relationships, it is a winter time to reflect deeply and place our trust in God. As in nature, winter is followed by new life in spring, so in our personal winters, springtime of new life will also return. We can be fully alive in every circumstance if we live in it with an attitude of trust and gratitude for whatever is.

We have wonderful examples of people who achieved it against all odds. Helen Keller comes to mind. Both blind and deaf from birth, with the persistence of her teacher, she learned to speak, write and become an inspiration for all physically challenged people and the rest of us too. There are examples in our own time and place. A 10-year-old child, bald from chemotherapy announced to a visitor at the hospital: "I have cancer, but I am fighting it."

A few years ago one of my young brothers died of cancer. When it was certain that he had less than four months he said, "I don't want to be dead before I die." So he continued to live fully doing the things he loved to do for as long as he could.

Other examples abound: "I love my life, I am so blessed!" a senior who survived a severe accident; the 98-year-old farmer putting in his 74th crop; young athletes striving to be the best they can be; students who have big dreams and study to be able to fulfill them.

Everyone who lives each moment to the best of their ability is fully alive. We all can list many examples in our own experience.

What are the signs of living fully? To live fully is to be in awe and amazement at the beauty and goodness around us. It is to live gratefully, seeing all as gift from our loving God. We can live fully only in the present. Yesterday is gone; tomorrow not yet here. The secret to fullness of life is to achieve the art of living in the now. I cannot change yesterday. I cannot do anything tomorrow until it becomes today. The only time that counts is the present. "Choose life so that you and your descendants may live, loving and obeying the Lord God," so we read in DEUTERONOMY 30:19. Choice is an action of today.

Our loving God lives in and among us. The more fully alive we are, the more glory we give to God.

All glory and praise to our God!
Amen

DEALING WITH LOSS

Writing and saving what is written can be tricky. I learned this to be true when I wrote an article, *What's in a Name?* It was a good article and I was sure I had saved it for future reference. But when I opened the file it was empty! No matter what I tried there was no way I could retrieve it. It was lost somewhere in cyber space and I was unable to find it. This was initially a very great loss for me. There is no way I can recreate the same thoughts and ideas. I felt deeply disappointed in my carelessness and even initially blamed my computer. Why had I not immediately made a hard copy as I always do? Then I reflected on what the loss means. Perhaps this was not what God wanted me to write about at this time. So I let go of it and relaxed.

Of course this little loss can hardly be compared with the great losses people are experiencing in floods and fire, earthquakes and tornados. Imagine losing home and everything in it by the fire. Imagine homes and contents flood-soaked beyond saving. Imagine the loss of countless lives in wars that need not be, if only we human beings could, would, talk to one another with respect for equal rights.

Imagine, too, the senseless loss of life and limb through highway accidents caused by carelessness or drunk driving. These are great losses that we, all of us in the human family care about. We may not have within us the spirit of Job whose famous words are familiar to us: "The Lord gave, and the Lord has taken away; blessed be the name of the Lord." (Job 1:21) But how can we deal with so much loss, our own and that of our sisters and brothers in the human family?

There are many kinds of loss; some may seem trivial; others are life changing in significant ways. The little daily losses may seem insignificant. Whatever the loss, each one needs to be grieved, yes even the loss of an article. My response to this loss was typical. At first I just couldn't believe or accept that it was really gone. Then I was upset with myself for being careless and also blamed my computer. I finally admitted and accepted that it was irretrievable; I started to make decisions about moving on. Then I found peace. Denial, anger, acceptance, new decision, these are stages most of us go through in dealing with loss.

We may ask, "Why me? Why now? What did I do to deserve this?" We may even be angry at God as well as with ourselves or someone close to us who 'should have helped to prevent this from happening to me'. All these responses are normal and acceptable. Then we take stock of the situation and discern our next course of action. Should I get a hearing aid? Is it best for me to move into an assisted living situation? Is it time to sell our home? We need not go it alone.

Prayer, seeking advice, sharing with family and friends are ways to ease the burden of decisions and leading to inner peace. The better we deal with the little losses the more prepared we are for the inevitable life changing loss of a loved one. We do know how to suffer loss; we need to trust our own insights. They are gifts from God who also trusts us. "Heed the counsel of your own heart, and above all pray to the Most High that you may be guided in the way of truth." (Ecclesiasticus 37:13,15) Perhaps we will eventually be able to join in Job's prayer: "The Lord gave, and the Lord has taken away; blessed be the name of the Lord!"

We have all experienced the greater loss in the death of loved ones. We know that we will all go through the same door from this life to the next. How do we think about death? What do we tell our children? What do our children tell us?

Both my parents have died. I learned some profound truths from some of our little ones. Eight-year-old great grandson, gazing reflectively at my dad in the coffin expressed this insight: "It looks like Grandpa is in a chrysalis and is going to be a butterfly!" Have you ever thought of a coffin as a chrysalis? And the butterfly is a beautiful symbol of resurrection and new life.

And a five-year-old great granddaughter wanted to see too. Lifted up by her granddad she went about seeing as little children do. This included touching, which she did, moving her hands over his face and hands, taking her time to really see. Then came her profound statement of what she saw. "He isn't here!"

With Jesus I pray, "I bless you Father, Lord of heaven and earth, for hiding these things from the learned and the clever and revealing them to mere children." (MATTHEW 11:25)

I learned another image of death from my mother. Several years before her death she put away her burial attire. It was a beautiful blue nightgown that she wrapped in plastic and labelled "for my burial." And she made sure we knew that she didn't want her glasses on in her coffin. "I never sleep with my glasses on." For her, death was eternal sleep, eternal rest. Of course she was buried minus her glasses wearing her beautiful blue nightgown.

May she and all who have died enjoy eternal rest in the arms of you
our loving God
Amen

WHERE IS HEAVEN?

Where do our loved ones go when they die? Where did Jesus go on Ascension when "a cloud took him out of their sight?" (Acts 1:9) We say "up in heaven," but where is up? In Australia the direction of up is opposite to ours. With space travel, the space station, our ever-expanding universe, we can see that Heaven is not a place in space. So where is Heaven?

Heaven is where God dwells and God is here and everywhere. Jesus speaks of the kingdom of God being among us. (Luke 17:21) As he commissions his disciples to go to all people everywhere with his message, he promises to be with them to the end of the age. God is not far from each one of us for "in him we live and move and have our being." (Acts 17:28) And in John 14:23, Jesus says, "Those who love me keep my word, and my Father will love them, and we will come to them and make our home with them."

What, then, is different for us when we die? Where are our loved ones who have died? They are with God in a new kind of life, a different mode of being. They are in eternity, no longer confined by time and space, but have entered a new frequency. They are free, unencumbered by the cares of this life. They live a new existence in communion with God and the angels and saints.

We hear of people who, as they approach death, see a parent or spouse ready to welcome them. Sometimes a person we were very close to comes to us. I was in a funeral home at the death of a friend's brother. I noticed four or five little children by the open coffin and joined them. They had questions about their grandfather and what was happening to him. A four-year-old girl said, "Grandpa is happy. He came to my room last night and told me I shouldn't be sad because he is happy." I believe that the child really experienced this encounter with her Grandpa. Do we not often feel our parents or other loved deceased close? They love us now more than ever and we can call on them to help us as we do other saints because they are in Heaven right around us.

Our Father who art in heaven
Thank you for making your home among us
Amen

PART THREE:
GOD'S GIFTS

BEAUTY IN VARIETY

Autumn is here in all its glory! Trees are exchanging their summer green for raiment of red, orange, gold, yellow and brown, giving a show of beauty in variety. They will, of course, shed these garments and stand naked in winter cold. Then their stark beauty reveals their skeletal shapes against the white of snow or sunny blue sky and occasionally they dress in robes of hoar frost. The seasons we in the northern hemisphere are privileged to experience offer another kind of variety, the circle of life. Autumn gives way to the sleep of winter only to awaken again to new life in spring and summer.

This reflection brings us to recognize how much God loves variety. The universe is full of unimaginable variety! Every star, every planet, moon, galaxy – all are unique creations of God, revealing his passionate love for variety.

Humanity, too, manifests the preference God has for variety. Within our own families and community there are great and small differences. Just look around when in the midst of a gathering of people. Worldwide there are differences in colour, race, creed, politics and values. Our Creator God made them all and loves them all unconditionally as his beloved children. God sees all that he has made and sees that it is very good.

Imagine a world where all the people are the same. They look the same with the same colouring and the same type of character. They all think and act the same. Absurd, isn't it?

WHO COULD STAND IT?

Years ago while studying scripture and theology with pastoral applications, I got into an argument with another student. I ended it by saying, "I'm glad I don't have to work with you." He responded, "On the contrary, if we were on the same team and agreed on everything, one of us would be superfluous!" Those words of wisdom have helped me in many conflicting situations. No one view can boast of being the full truth with nothing to learn from other views. Conflicts in families, committees, communities can usually be resolved by trying to understand the other side(s). It is much more interesting and more enjoyable to live in situations that are rich with a variety of ideas. Now if only leaders of nations would recognize that there is more than one way to settle differences.

Little children are naturally accepting of differences. A coal-black boy and his family moved into the neighborhood. During the summer little Jennifer played with Brucie and they became friends. On the first day of school Jennifer's mom worried that the other children would tease Brucie. However, when Jennifer returned from her first day in kindergarten she said, "Do you know who has the bestes' tan in the whole class? Brucie."

No wonder Jesus said, "Unless you change and become like children, you will never enter the kingdom." (MATTHEW 18:3) Would that we adults would be like them in their acceptance and joy with differences instead of teaching them to be judgmental and discriminatory like we are.

May we learn to trust that our Creator God knows what is best for us and celebrate the gift of beauty in variety.

> *All you works of God, praise our God*
>
> *Sun and moon, and stars of heaven, sing praise with the heavenly host*
>
> *Let all the Earth bless our God*
>
> *Praise and exalt God above all forever*
>
> *Amen*
>
> (EXCERPTS FROM DANIEL 3)

HANDS

On Ascension Sunday, I, along with Sister Petra, had the privilege of welcoming parishioners to our Sunday celebration. I clasped all kinds of hands:

Hands that were used to hard physical labour;

The soft gentle hands of mothers;

Hands with fingers missing and a story to tell;

The little hands of shy children;

Cold hands and warm hands;

Old wrinkled hands with wisdom stories to tell;

Your hands and my hands.

At communion we stretched out these same hands to receive and become Body of Christ. Ours are the only hands Christ has to continue his work of spreading the reign of God.

How do our hands become the hands Christ uses?

Every touch, every caress, every hand that toils; every hand that cooks and washes dishes; hands that take care of creation by raking, seeding, pruning; hands that are clasped in reconciliation; hands that bless, that write, that do homework, that play ball or piano.

All that we do with our hands that is loving, caring, creative, supportive – these are ways in which we act as Body of Christ. When we do such Godlike things with our hands, Christ is proud to call us disciples and friends.

Thank you, God, for our hands that can do so many diverse things

thanks, too, for the insight to use them

to continue Christ's mission wherever we are

Amen

GROUNDED IN EUCHARIST

A seed planted, warmed by the sun and watered by the rain, dies to its own being, becomes rooted, and then grows into a plant of its own kind.

To be grounded in Eucharist is to be planted into the dying of Jesus, become rooted in the depths of his self-gift and so bud forth Eucharist for nourishment and life.

As the seed gives itself up to the soil, dies to its own being, so we are called to let go, to surrender ourselves to be planted in the act of Christ's dying.

His was an act of total self-gift, total surrender to the Father whose will he sought above all, and by whom he felt abandoned. "My God, my God, why have you forsaken me?" In that moment of utter aloneness he cried out in trust and leapt into the darkness of death, and therefore was caught up in the eternal embrace of the Father and given the name above all names—Jesus, Lord.

In Eucharist, he unites our self-surrender with his, offers it to the Father, and makes it fruitful. Eucharist urges us to lay down our lives.

At the Eucharistic celebration we dare to stretch out our hand to receive the Body of Christ. The opening of the hand is an act of self-surrender. Amen! Yes! I give myself to become Body of Christ, broken, shared and given. To dare to stretch out my hand in communion is to dare to risk it all, to welcome insecurity, to walk his way in radical discipleship.

The seed that gives itself up to the soil, dying to its own being, comes alive. It sends roots into the earth to be anchored, given a source of strength and stability.

Eucharist is the centre of our life of faith. The sharing of this body and blood in this sacrificial meal unites us more intensely with Jesus and our sisters and brothers. Jesus prayed for our oneness in him, "That all may be one, as you, Father, and I are one."

United with Christ who is in the eternal embrace of the Father, we are strong with his strength, filled with his Spirit, nourished by his self-gift.

At the Eucharistic celebration we dare to stretch out our hand and be united in the Body of Christ. The opening of the hand is an act of acceptance. Amen! Yes! I receive and become one with the Body of Christ, my sisters and brothers, all, broken and bleeding, shared and lonely, lovable and unlovely. To dare to stretch out my hand in communion is to dare to accept and share the gifts and weaknesses, the goodness and sinfulness, the dignity and shame of others, and to ask them to share mine.

In memory of Jesus and following his example, we are impelled to extend Eucharist into our daily lives, giving ourselves totally for others, gratefully receiving from them.

The seed that is rooted, sprouts and grows into a plant, bearing fruit of its own kind.

Grounded in Eucharist we bud forth, grow to be more and more one with the Lord and bear his fruit, the Bread of Life, Eucharist. In Eucharist he unites our self-surrender with his, offers it to the Father and makes it fruitful.

Daily we are challenged to "DO THIS" in his memory. "Do what I do," we can imagine Jesus saying. "Take your body, your time and energy, break it, share it, be present in live-giving concern. Pour out your blood, your life, in a new covenant which is forever. Be faithful in a world that knows little fidelity. Be life, be nourishment. RE-MEM-BER ME."

At the Eucharistic celebration we dare to stretch out our hand in communion to receive all in order to give all. My open hand says, "Here I am, Lord, send me." To open my hand is to dare to believe that God gifts me, strengthens me, loves me and sends me. To stretch out my hand in communion is to stretch out my hand in service.

Eucharist is the strongest impetus and challenge to be about the mission of Jesus.

Lord Jesus feed us with your love and life

May your self-gift give us the courage and generosity

To give of ourselves for others

Amen

LORD, THAT I MAY SEE!

Recent eye surgery gave me occasion to reflect on this prayer of the blind man. I came to appreciate the gift of eyesight, one of God's wonderful creations. Lord, that I may see as you see. When creating the universe, our planet Earth with all its life forms, "God saw that it was good." (GENESIS 1:25) Do I, do we, see our entire Earth home as good? Surely then we would take care of it as the treasure it is, with all its variety of colour and natural beauty.

When God created humankind, male and female, in his own image, "God saw everything that he had made and indeed it was very good." (Gen. 1:31) We see and experience the great gift of the human body and spirit. During the recent Olympics, did we not rejoice at its beauty in the ice-dancing, the strength and flexibility in figure-skating, the skill and daring maneuvers of the skiers? Were we not proud that members of the human family, our family, could challenge one another in the various games and events with fairness and respect? And God also saw that it was very good.

Lord, that I may see my sisters and brothers all over the world as you see them.

You look on each one of us with love and compassion.

That is how I desire to see others, nonjudgmentally with love and compassion.

Sometimes we see great devastation, wars, murders, the buying and selling of human beings. God also sees the sinfulness and always calls for conversion and is ready to forgive. And once forgiven remembers no more. After the sin and devastation the Israelites experienced, God said, "Do not remember the former things or consider the things of old. I am about to do a new thing; now it springs forth; do you not perceive it? (ISAIAH 43:18-19) The new thing that God accomplishes is loving the world so much that he sends his only Son to save us. We are in the midst of recalling and celebrating this new thing of Paschal Mystery. May we open our eyes, minds and hearts to perceive and experience God's unconditional love in Jesus Christ.

Speaking to his disciples, Jesus told them, "Blessed are the eyes that see what you see. For I tell you that many prophets and kings desired to see what you see, but did not see it, and to hear what you hear, but did not hear it." (LUKE 10:23-24) We are among the disciples whose eyes are blessed to see, if only we desire to see whatever God shows us.

Lord

That we may see all that you reveal to us

Amen

LIFE IS CHANGE

We live in change. Sometimes we may wonder, "Why can't anything stay the same? Life as it is or was, was comfortable. I knew where and how I fit in, what was to happen next." But no, every morning I wake up to a new day and I am a day older. Everything and everyone is always in flux. Nature is always changing. If trees and flowers, birds and animals always stayed the same they would be artificial, a work of human art, but certainly not real. Whatever lives is in a state of constant change.

People, too, are always changing. We are born; we grow and go to school; we eventually leave home to our grownup life. We start our own family and the cycle starts all over again. We age and mature and grow old with all kinds of physical, mental and spiritual changes. Eventually we die. But even this is not the end. Our Christian faith tells us that in death our life is changed, not taken away. As children of God's most precious creation, what is our role in managing the changes according to God's design? What kinds of decisions are ours to make so that our life becomes and is the special gift of our loving Creator? Ours is a vital role in God's ongoing creation.

How God must love variety with the ever changing works of his creation, including us! We have no control about getting older. Because the days and years proceed as God planned, aging takes no effort on our part. It just happens. The kind of person we become depends on the choices we make. We are entrusted with the gift of life and the gift of time during which to mold and develop the precious person we are created to be. What a blessing that we have one constant in our life on which we can depend.

God, who is always doing something new, never changes. His love is eternal and unconditional. I imagine God delighting in surprising us with every new and wonderful way he shows his love. "I am about to do a new thing; now it springs forth; do you not perceive it?" (ISAIAH 43:19)

Loving Creator God
Help us to see all the beauty and life around us
the daily gift of your creativity
All glory and praise to you
Amen

GOD'S FAMILY TREE

Family trees are popular, interesting and necessary to know fully who we are. Our family tree tells us our origin and helps us discover relatives we never knew. I have a copy of my family tree with my great grandparents as the root. According to this tree, I am fourth generation. Fourth and fifth generation photos are special news and published in local newspapers. Longevity is at play here. It seems important to know our ancestry to help us know ourselves, as well as discovering a widening circle of relatives.

We have been celebrating the mystery of God's only Son in whom God is well pleased. Because Jesus Christ came to live among us, becoming one with us, sharing our humanity, we, too, are daughters and sons of the same God. "See what the Father has given us that we should be called children of God; and that is what we are." (1 JOHN 3:1) All of us are God's beloved children. There are no generations in God's family tree as in our own. Every one of us is first generation, sharing with Christ in the immediate family of God. God has no grandchildren.

St. Paul writes: "We are children of God, and if children, then heirs, heirs of God and joint heirs with Christ." (ROMANS 8:17) Of the human race, who all is included? Paul writes in EPHESIANS 3:6, "The Gentiles have become fellow heirs, members of the same body, and sharers in the promise in Christ Jesus through the gospel." The whole human race, no matter the colour of their skin, or their traditions and beliefs, all are children of the same loving God. And all deserve our respect, our caring, our love, since all are our brothers and sisters, beloved children of God.

> Eckhart von Hochheim, commonly known as Meister Eckhart, was a German theologian, philosopher and mystic who lived in the 13th century in Germany.

This touches the very mystery of who God is as a trinity of persons giving life to the world.

The mystic, Meister Eckhart, describes our origin in the Trinity in the following prayer. Only a mystic could come up with a description like this. To me it says that Our Creator joyfully gives birth to us, all of us. Should we not, then, be joyful people?

In the core of the Trinity the Father laughs and gives birth to the Son
In the core of the Trinity the Son laughs back and gives birth to the Spirit
In the core of the Trinity they all laugh and give birth to us
Amen

PART FOUR:
OUR LIFE IN GOD

CHOOSE LIFE

I have set before you, life and death, blessings and curses. Choose life so that you and your descendants may live, loving the Lord your God, obeying him and holding fast to him.

(DEUTERONOMY 30:19)

Jesus came that we may have life, life to the full. (JOHN 10:10)

"Choose life!" says our loving God who created us in God's image. "Live life to the full, for that is why I came," says Jesus. May all our daily choices enhance our life so that we become the person God created us to be. We all have the freedom and the right to make choices that are right and good for us. With the right and freedom comes responsibility. Choosing life means "obeying and holding fast to God." Sometimes our personal boundaries are violated so that we feel that we have no choices left. But we do. God has created us equal and gifted each one with free will and conscience to choose well.

"Choose life!" says our triune God to every family. May all your family choices enhance the life of your family as a whole as well as that of each member. Live your family life fully in peace, harmony and loving service of one another, so that every family shares in the love and unity of God, Father, Son and Holy Spirit.

"Choose life!" says our loving God to our community. *"Enjoy it to the full,"* says Jesus. "Remember that is why I came." May the choices of every person and the participation of every family enhance the life of the community as a whole as well as that of every family and that of every citizen.

May the decisions of community leaders and all who serve in public life contribute to the well-being of all the people. St. Irenaeus assures us that the Glory of God is the human person fully alive! This prayer is adapted from *Wishes* by Lynn Robbins.

God of life, let me not sleep through half my life

Let me know the real joy of being alive

Let me see it as the marvelous gift that it is

Help me live my life fully

Let me trust that it is good to honour you by being the special person I was always meant to be

Amen

PRAYING THE NEWS

Do you ever wonder what to do with your feelings as you watch the daily newscasts? Sometimes I feel angry at the stupidity of (grown up?) politicians. I feel sad at the violence perpetrated by youth on youth. I wonder why centuries of wars between peoples haven't yet convinced the leaders and populace that wars just don't work. I feel betrayed by our church at the abuses of children by priests. I am stymied at the greed of men who buy and sell human beings, mostly women and children, for sexual gratification and fat bank accounts. I am filled with pity for the victims of natural disasters. This list could be even longer. Sometimes I wonder if I should even bother learning what is going on in our world.

I decided to try praying the news instead of just watching it. How is this done?

At the stupidity of politicians and others, I ask the Spirit of wisdom to enter their hearts and pray for myself to be less judgmental. I ask our loving God to send someone loving into the lives of youths and children, someone who will love them unconditionally with God's own love. I pray for the conversion of church leaders and all who use their positions of authority or superiority to abuse the little ones. I pray for healing for all who suffer from addictions of any kind. I pray for the repose of the souls of the victims of suicide bombings and natural disasters. This way of watching the news is much easier on my nerves and gives me personal peace of mind and heart.

What is most important of all is to send positive vibes into our universe. Every positive thought, word and deed increases the overall spirit in the whole world. The opposite is also true. Negativity breeds negativity. Loving, peaceful thoughts produce more loving and peaceful spirits. This is borne out for me every time I walk to the post office or store. People smile and greet one another and ask how you are. There is a positive spirit that I am sure is enhanced by every smile, kind word and helpful action. I believe we live what the sign on the highway east of my town says...

Behold, how pleasant it is for brothers and sisters to live together in Unity!
Amen

HOW WE PRAY

A man was asked to pray for a favourite aunt. He agreed to do so saying, "She prayed for me, so I guess I should pray for her. But I won't say words; I'll just think." Was just 'thinking' real prayer? Of course. God doesn't need words, we do. God reads hearts and thoughts as well as hearing our words.

There are many ways of praying. When his disciples asked Jesus to teach them, he gave them the Our Father. This continues to be a favourite prayer among Christians. Jesus would go "up the mountain by himself to pray." (MATTHEW 19:23) While there did he pray the Our Father? Or psalms? Or was he simply silently in the presence of his Abba with love and openness? However Jesus prayed it inspired his followers to learn from him.

We find many examples of prayer in scripture. God says in JEREMIAH 29:12-13, "When you call upon me and come and pray to me, I will hear you. If you seek me with all your heart, I will let you find me." In MATTHEW 6, Jesus teaches much about prayer besides the Our Father. "Whenever you pray, go to your room and shut the door and pray to your Father who is in secret; and your Father who sees in secret will reward you." "Whatever you ask for in prayer, believe that you have received it, and it will be yours." (MARK 11:24) This saying brings to mind a grade one student I had many years ago. During a lesson on prayer he asked, "Doeth God alwayth anther our prayer? I have been praying for yearth and yearth and yearth for a little brother and thtill don't have one." There are times when our prayers of request need others to pray with us. In the case of this six-year-old his parents could have helped him pray for a little brother.

Rosary
A form of devotion to the Virgin Mary, chiefly consisting of three sets of five decades each of the Hail Mary, each decade preceded by the Lord's Prayer and ending with a Glory Be...

There are many ways of praying. In oral prayer we use the words of common prayer, the Our Father, psalms, rosary, to name a few. We may also use our own words in speaking to our loving God. In meditation we may read a passage in scripture or ponder an event in our life and reflect on what God is saying through this event or Word from scripture.

Contemplation is entering into the solitude of our heart where God dwells. We may choose a mantra to keep us attuned and let God speak to us. Just walking in the presence of God is a simple form of contemplation, being aware of his presence in nature, in the face of a child, in the love we experience.

We may find at times that we just can't pray. We are dry and even uninterested to keep on trying. Then, as St. Paul assures us, "The Spirit helps us in our weakness; for we do not know how to pray as we ought, but that very Spirit intercedes with sighs too deep for words. And God, who searches the heart, knows what is the mind of the Spirit, because the Spirit intercedes for us." (ROMANS 8:26-27) The great mystic, St. Theresa of Avila, says that no matter how much we have developed our prayer life, we all should at times become beginners again.

Let us persevere in prayer, whether with words or just 'thinking,' alone in secret or with family and within our faith community. God will hear us and speak to us, for God is LOVE.

Thank you God for always hearing our prayers

Amen

THE GOOD SAMARITAN

Jesus often used parables in his teaching. These stories helped to clarify and illustrate the message he was giving. Each parable has deeper meaning than just the story line. God and we are often meant to be the characters in the story. The Good Samaritan is such a parable. (LUKE 10:25FF)

A lawyer really knew the answer before he asked the question: "What must I do to inherit eternal life?" We also know the answer to love God and neighbor. We also know the answer Jesus gave, "Do this and you will live." To cover up his embarrassment the lawyer asked the crucial question, "Who is my neighbor?" which gave Jesus the opportunity to tell a story.

A traveler was attacked and robbed and left half dead in the ditch. The one who helped him was a despised Samaritan. He truly was a good neighbor. The lawyer is challenged to do likewise. On the obvious level of the story, we, too, are challenged to love others without prejudice. It is the only way we obey the greatest commandment to love God and neighbor as our self.

However, we can dig deeper into this parable. While on retreat at Queen's House in Saskatoon, the priest helped us see ourselves and God in this story. Who is the person lying half dead in the gutter? Perhaps it is someone who needs our help, needs us to be the Good Samaritan. Or perhaps it is you or I who are living as though we were half dead or half alive. Who or what robs us of what is needed to live fully? We may be tired and sick. We may be lonely, despondent, lacking motivation. These and other conditions may be the robbers who keep us from living fully. "The glory of God is the human person fully alive!"

If I am the person in the ditch who is the Good Samaritan? Is it not God who so loved the world that he gave his only Son that all who believe will have eternal life? (JOHN 3:16) And the one who was sent, Jesus the Christ, asserts, "I have come that you may have life and have it to the full." (JOHN 10:10) So whatever keeps me from being fully alive can be healed by the Good Samaritan who is Jesus Christ.

At the end of his conversation with the lawyer Jesus exhorts him to "go and do likewise." That is, be a good neighbor to whoever needs help. This is also meant for us. This deeper level of meaning translates into doing as Jesus Christ does.

Jesus

help me be a good Samaritan whenever I see a person in need

Amen

THE ROYAL VISIT

An often heard comment in the media was, "They are so ordinary, just like us." Of course they are. They are part of the human race. As we do, Will and Kate share our common human nature, even as Jesus also does. We are both limited and dying, and limitless into eternal life. Yes, Will and Kate are Duke and Duchess. They are 'royal' for some of the human race. But it isn't this kind of royalty that makes them so admired, so ordinary, so like us.

There is another Royal visiting us, not just visiting, but staying with us always, Jesus Christ, PRINCE of PEACE. And we share in his royalty, because "God so loved the world that that he gave his only Son, so that everyone who believes in him...may have eternal life." (JOHN 3:16) St. Peter writes that we are a chosen people, a royal priesthood, a holy people. (1 PETER 2:9) Through this Prince of Peace, we share in the very life of God. So do all Christians, and also Prince William and Katherine.

Did the royal visit make a difference in the lives of Canadians, and even in all the world who tuned in to all their activities, their interactions and their words? Perhaps. But we know that our Prince who is with us, intimately involved in our life, loves us unconditionally; this Prince not only makes a difference, he is our life. After all, he came that we may have life, life to the full, and he says of himself: "I am the Way, the Truth and the Life." Through Jesus, God shares our humanity. And we share in God's divine life.

How in our daily life does Jesus Christ make a difference? How is life different for us because of him? How is my life changed since I have come to know and love God? God is my constant companion. More than that, God lives within and around me and I in God. In ACTS 17:28, we are told, and I believe, "In him we live and move and have our being." I chose to live this life by following my vocation as a School Sister of Notre Dame. I live this life within community which is the Body of Christ and am nurtured by the faith community wherever I live and serve.

Each member of the Body of Christ, the community of believers, is very much influenced by being part of the royal family of the Prince of Peace. Each person has a unique and personal response to the invitation to "live and move" within the community, the Body of Christ, the Royal family of God. How is your personal life of faith affected by your call through baptism? How is Jesus Christ present in your family life? Does each one of us truly believe in the depths of our hearts that we are royal children of God whose eternal home is the kingdom of God we call heaven? It is our heritage. May we rejoice as we greet each other at our final grand family reunion!

God our Father. Thank you for inviting us into your family
with Jesus as our brother.
May our small reunions here and now
prepare us for the grand eternal reunion
Amen

ALL ARE INVITED

It is Sunday morning. No matter the weather or temperatures, people are gathering. We can see families walking, carrying their little ones; others leaving their cars and converging at their church for Sunday celebration. This sight brings to mind the Carey Landry hymn: The Spirit is a-movin' all over this land ... and people are gathering, the church is born....

As we gather we greet one another, happy to meet again as faith family. We sing God's praises, proclaim the Word of God, and reflect on the message for the new week just begun. We ask forgiveness for our sinfulness, knowing that our all-loving God receives our repentance and affirms our status as his children. As a community we renew our faith in God our Creator and loving Father, in Jesus our Saviour and Brother, in the Spirit giving birth to our church and in life everlasting. We lift up to our merciful God our concerns and needs. We pray for the sick among us, for our families and community, for world peace, and for whatever worries us. We trust that our caring God hears and answers us in good time.

We remember the life, death and resurrection of Jesus, our Saviour and Brother. In communion we share in his Body and Blood. In doing so we become the Body of Christ, his way of being present in the world. "Now you are the body of Christ and individually members of it." (COLOSSIANS 1:18) And in COLOSSIANS 12:12 we read: "For just as the body is one and has many members...so it is with Christ. For in one Spirit we were all baptized into one body..."

Finally we are sent out with blessing and song to live anew what we have celebrated.

These Sunday gatherings are joyful meetings. By our baptism we have a standing invitation. By our presence we strengthen and enrich the gathered community. We are all needed to complete the family circle.

Unfortunately there are those among us who either do not know or believe the invitation that is offered them. Just as every member of our bodies is necessary for its proper functioning, so too is every member of the Body of Christ which we are by our baptism. As St. Paul writes in 1 CORINTHIANS 12:12, "For just as the body is one and has many members, and all the members of the body, though many, are one body, so it is with Christ."

We have heard the excuses: *"I can pray better in nature, on the golf course, at home."*

It is hoped that all of us heed the need to pray in all those places. Jesus said to pray always and to go to our room and shut the door. But these prayer times cannot replace the community Sunday worship.

"They are all hypocrites who go to church. Holy, holy on Sunday and then...?"

I am not aware of hypocrites in church or at home, but I do know that all who go to church know that they are sinners and in need of God and community.

"I don't get anything out of church. It is so boring."

Perhaps if you participate, sing along, take part in ministries such as proclaiming the Word, joining the choir, and simply give it your all, you and the whole community will be the richer.

We receive this invitation from Jesus: *"You are invited to my party, my banquet next Sunday. RSVP."*

Thank you, Jesus, for inviting me
Give me the desire and willpower to respond
"Yes, Jesus, I will come"

SPIRITUALITY

Spirituality is our life in the Spirit, our habitual relationship with our loving God who dwells in us and we in God. (JOHN 14) There are many practices and prayer types that help our growth in this relationship with our triune God. For example: the rosary, novenas, daily morning and night prayer, meditation. Most important of all we have the sacraments—especially the Eucharist. All of these and many more practices are good and holy, leading to deeper intimacy with God.

Some practices can become hindrances to our spiritual growth. This is true when we place more faith and trust in the practice than in God, like the Pharisee in Jesus' parable. Two men went to the temple to pray—one a Pharisee; the other a tax collector. The Pharisee enumerated his good practices: He fasted twice a week and he gave 10 percent of his earnings to charity. These were good practices which could have deepened his relationship with God. However, in his pride he relied on the practices to justify him. He even prayed, "God, I thank you that I am not like other people, including this tax collector." In the meantime the tax collector simply prayed for mercy, and Jesus says, "This man went home justified rather than the other." (LUKE 18: 9FF)

We could also fall into the trap of overconfidence in what WE do, not realizing that our trust may be in our fidelity to a practice rather than on God. For example: We sometimes make what we call novenas. For nine consecutive days (or weeks or months) we use a specified prayer or practice for a special intention. This is a holy and laudable practice. Suppose an emergency of some kind, perhaps a child or neighbor needs attention in the middle of this novena. Do I start over believing that it won't work if I miss this one day for another's need? This could be having more faith in the nine days than trusting in God who doesn't bother counting but looks at the heart.

There are various practices and ways of spending time in prayer, some of them may be adapted from other religions and cultures, and from nature. If they are good and helpful, they are from God who created all people to be in relationship with him.

Quietly sitting in meditation, aware of being in the presence of the most Holy One who lives within is a wonderfully peaceful practice. Praying the psalms, remembering that Jesus also prayed these very hymns, joining a prayer group, praying as family, all these are ways to nourish our spiritual life.

Hymns and psalms are interchangeable terms and both can be said or sung.

Jesus gave us good example; he went off by himself to pray; and teaching: Whenever you pray, do not be like the hypocrites; for they stand and pray in the synagogues and at the street corners, so that they may be seen by others... But whenever you pray, go to your room and shut the door, and pray to your Father who is in secret; and your Father who sees in secret will reward you... When you are praying, do not heap up empty phrases as the Gentiles do; for they think that they will be heard because of their many words...Pray then in this way: our Father, etc. (MATTHEW 6:5FF)

Let us live with our God in whatever way we are Spirit-led. May we all continue in faithful practice of our faith and pray for one another.

FORGIVENESS, GIFT OF GOD'S LOVE

There is a story of an old Cherokee Indian telling his grandson about a battle that goes on inside people.

He said, "My son, the battle is between two wolves inside us all. One is Evil. It is anger, envy, sorrow, regret, greed, arrogance, self-pity, guilt, resentment, inferiority, lies, false pride, superiority, and ego.

The other is Good. It is joy, peace, love, hope, serenity, humility, kindness, benevolence, empathy, generosity, truth, compassion and faith." The grandson thought about it for a minute and then asked his grandfather, "Which wolf wins?" The old Cherokee simply replied, "The one you feed."

St. Paul describes a similar inner conflict he experiences. "I do not do the good I want, but the evil I do not want...Wretched man that I am! Who will rescue me? Thanks be to God, through Jesus Christ our Lord." (Romans 7:24-25)

How do we feed either one of these 'wolves' inside us? I believe we feed the Evil one best by holding on to grudges, hurts, anger, refusing to let go and move on. It seems that it is in our nature, as St. Paul described, to sometimes or often, hurt one another, make mistakes, do or say stupid things to one another...really mess up. Is there anyone who has never been hurt by someone close? Or is there anyone who has never hurt another person in word or action? Hang on to all of it and feed the evil wolf.

But if we forgive by letting go of grudges and bitterness and anger, we are led down the path of healing and peace. When we embrace forgiveness we embrace peace, hope, gratitude, joy. When I forgive someone, I set a prisoner free and discover that the prisoner is none other than I, myself.

Of course, as St. Paul acknowledges, we need to cry out for someone to rescue us from ourselves. Our first action is to pray for forgiveness and God answers, "I will forgive their iniquity, and remember their sin no more." (Jeremiah 31:34)

So, God can forgive, but how can I? "To err is human, to forgive is divine." When Jesus forgave the paralytic, he was criticized because, "Who can forgive sins but God alone?" (Mark 2:7) And yet God requires of us that we forgive those who have hurt us. In the prayer Jesus himself taught, we pray, "Forgive us our trespasses as we forgive those who trespass against us."

When Peter asked Jesus how many times he is required to forgive, Jesus told him seventy seven times, that is, don't bother counting – forgive every time. Jesus gave the ultimate example on the cross when he prayed, "Father, forgive them, they know not what they do." It is for this forgiveness and mercy that God loved the world so much that he sent his Son to be our forgiveness. God's unconditional love forgives when we contritely open our hearts to change. And we share in the mission of forgiving that brings such peace. Forgiveness will change bitterness and anger into love.

That is how we are at our best as image of God.

Forgive us our trespasses as we forgive those who trespass against us

Amen

LIFE AFTER DEATH

Who of us has not lost a loved one: parent, spouse, child, best friend? Every community has its fair share of funerals. We join in this good-bye ritual in support of the mourners. We pray for the deceased, knowing and believing that they will live again. By our presence, our prayers, our hugs and words of condolence, we support the grieving. There is a story about an old man who had just lost his long-time wife. He was sitting alone on his porch swing. The neighbor's little boy, seeing how sad and lonely he was, went over and sat with him for a while. When he returned his mom asked, "What did you talk about?" "We didn't talk. I just helped him cry."

When a loved one dies, it is normal to feel we could have done more, been there to say good-bye and I love you. We wonder if there is some unfinished word or action that we could have done. We ask a thousand "what ifs." But the fact is that the act of dying is a solo flight into the arms of our all-loving God. It is the last act of obedience to God's call.

We are left to grieve and pray for eternal rest for our loved one. Because we believe they will rise again, we know that it is "a holy and pious thought" to pray for the dead. (2 Maccabees 12:45) When we pray the creed we affirm that we believe "in the resurrection of the body and life everlasting." (Apostles Creed) We have assurance of this also in Revelations 21:36-45: *"And God himself will wipe away every tear from our eyes. Death will be no more. See, I am making all things new."*

Apostles Creed
A Christian statement of belief ascribed to the Twelve Apostles and used especially in public worship.

In the meantime, our grieving hurts and tears flow. The death of one so close to us leaves a big hole in our lives. Weeping is one form of healing the loss. Jesus wept at the tomb of his friend Lazarus. By our faith, we know that the communion of saints includes our deceased loved ones and ourselves. We ask saints to intercede for us. We may also ask our loved ones to pray for us. And about any unfinished words or actions, we can talk it over with them, tell of your love and ask for forgiveness for any hurts you gave them. It is comforting to talk to them and feel their closeness. And in one as yet unknown day, we will be with them for all eternity.

I believe in the communion of saints
the forgiveness of sins
and life everlasting
Amen

PART FIVE:
LIVING WHAT
WE BELIEVE

LET'S CELEBRATE CREATION

In the beginning God created the heavens and the earth. Now the earth was a formless void, there was darkness over the deep, and God's spirit hovered over the water. (Gen.1:1)

Chapters 1 and 2 in Genesis describe two versions of how God created everything that is. And everything that is, God sees as good; human beings, as very good.

Summer is a time when we enjoy the richness of our home, Planet Earth. What is our relationship with it? This relationship has undergone various stages in history. From the Genesis story we learned that Earth was arranged in hierarchical order: angels, men, women, children, animals, plants, rocks. We humans were spiritual with souls; everything else was for our use. I believe most of us no longer buy wholeheartedly into this view.

Then there is a materialistic world view. The spiritual realm where God dwells is above Earth, and Earth is nothing but stuff, matter. Our human role, our work is to control it. Earth is a resource which we could use or destroy. We have done both quite well.

Are we not now in, or moving toward, a worldview that is more ecological? We are one with all that is. Scientifically we are made of the same stuff, matter of which all created things are made. We are made of star dust. We are intimately interrelated, interdependent with the plants, animals and minerals, with water, air and soil. In this worldview our role changes. "Our Great Work now...is to carry out the transition from a period of human devastation of the Earth to a period when humans would be present to the planet in a mutually enhancing manner" (Thomas Berry, priest, eco-theologian, Earth scholar, author).

We are coming to realize that "The Earth is much more sacred than we have supposed, much holier than we have treated it. It is not only the human that has spirit. There has been spirit hovering over all the world since the beginning of creation" (Vincent Donovan, author, *The Church in the Midst of Creation*).

Chief Seattle's message in 1854 has good advice for us today. I quote a few excerpts:

> "You must teach your children that the ground beneath their feet is the ashes of our ancestors. So that they will respect the land, tell your children that the earth is rich with the lives of our kin.
>
> The earth does not belong to the human; the human belongs to the earth. All things are connected. Whatever befalls the earth, befalls the sons and daughters of earth.
>
> This earth is precious to God."

As we enjoy the gift of summer with picnics, swimming, gardening, camping, haying, holidaying, may we, who are "very good," remember to care for this precious Earth and praise God who created it and keeps it in existence.

Bless the Lord, O my soul
Lord my God, you are very great
You are clothed with honour and majesty
wrapped in light as with a garment
O Lord, how manifold are your works! In wisdom you have made them all
the Earth is full of your creatures
I will sing praise to my God while I have being
May my meditation be pleasing to God for I rejoice in the Lord
(Psalm 104, selected verses)

THE SEASONS OF LIFE

In September we welcome the first day of autumn. It is the day when our Earth's tilt creates equal hours of light and dark, the time of equal day and night. This change of season invites reflection on our own seasons of life.

"For everything there is a season," we read in ECCLESIASTES 3:1-8.

During this season of nature, we harvest our fields and gardens, making all things ready for the darkening time of winter. This is a time of maturity, of fruitfulness, of surrender, as trees and fields are stripped of all signs of life. In our life, too we experience autumn times when we harvest the wisdom that years have given us, when we are confronted with situations demanding surrender of loved ones, or health, or energies. Then we can learn from the season of autumn that out of surrender, out of dying comes new life.

We live all the seasons in different ways. When we are born and grow through childhood and adolescence we are in the springtime of life. As we mature in body and spirit and give life and nurture it, as we are fruitful by the work of our hands and minds, as we are successful in careers and family, we are enjoying the abundance of summer. Like the summer in nature, ours has calm and peaceful times as well as stormy ones. When our children leave home, experiencing their own summertime, as we begin to feel the aches and pains of waning health and vigour, as life asks us more and more to surrender what we have known, we are in our autumn season. But along with the losses we also enjoy the harvest of wisdom life has taught us. We enjoy the freedom of birds flying south, the colourful variety of children and grandchildren and our hearts are in a perpetual state of thanksgiving. We then begin our winter season, the time of life that sometimes seems useless. We are on the final lap of life's journey. But we know and believe that our ending in this life is but a beginning of life eternal.

However, we experience different seasons at various times in our lives. In our seventies or eighties we can experience spring as we rejoice at the birth of a grandchild, or receive the good news of renewed health and vigour. At any age we experience winter at the death of a loved one, or the loss of a job and livelihood. The cycle of the seasons speaks to us of the circle of life–death–life that we experience in our own lives. Everything that dies also gives life. Everything that lives also dies to live again.

The changing seasons in nature can teach us about the call to continual change, growth and transformation in our own lives. The more we reverence Earth in all her wonders and live in tune with her rhythms, the more whole we become in the way we live.

Let us welcome this beautiful season of autumn in the words of author Edward Hayes in *Prayers of a Planetary Pilgrim*:

> *Welcome, autumn, arms full of summer's blessings, carrying seeds of life*
> *for next year's planting*
> *Welcome, Old Wise One, may I be your student in the school of gratitude*
> *Guide me in reflecting upon summer now gone*
> *that I might give thanks for all the many gifts that have enriched me*
> *in the season of growth*
> *The heavens (and earth) are telling the glory of God!*
>
> (PSALM 19:1)

IS PEACE POSSIBLE?

What is happening in our world? It seems that nations choose sides, teams, as it were, in the game of life. The goal of this game appears to be to wipe each other off the face of the Earth. No one is spared. Women and little children and the old and sick as well as those wielding weapons or throwing stones, all are killed by the other side. Besides these wars, there is starvation all kinds of abuse of women and children. There is hoarding of wealth while others are homeless and dying of disease and starvation.

I have made a practice of praying the news, watching with God, asking God to bless, send wisdom, intervene, anything to make the madness stop. "God, how and why do you still put up with us, still loving us unconditionally? Is there anything I, we can do to help change our world for the better?" And God's Word in scripture has the answer. His is a message of love and peace, challenging his children to follow his lead.

In DEUTERONOMY 20:10, there is this surprising line in the midst of rules of war: "When you draw near to a town to fight against it, offer it terms of peace." What would it be like if the warring factions around the world would offer terms of peace? What if people in our families and communities would look for peaceful ways to solve differences? In LEVITICUS 26:3, God asks obedience of us, keeping all his commandments. If we do so: "I will grant peace in the land...."(verse 6) Jesus tells us that the greatest commandments and encompassing all others are, "Love the Lord your God with all your heart, and with all your soul, and with all your mind. This is the greatest and first commandment. And the second is like it: You shall love your neighbor as yourself." (MATTHEW 22:37-39) And in MARK 10:50 Jesus says, "Be at peace with one another."

St. Paul, in 1 CORINTHIANS 10:32, adds his words of wisdom: "Give no offense to Jew or Greek or to the church of God." In other words, just don't offend anyone. In ROMANS 14:19 he gives this advice: "Let us pursue what makes for peace and for mutual up building." Have you heard of the butterfly effect? It is said that due to weather processes, a butterfly flapping its wings in Tahiti can, in theory, produce a tornado in Kansas. Let us not underestimate the power of our loving thoughts, words and actions to create a better atmosphere among peoples everywhere.

We will certainly make our own homes and community better, happier than they already are. Our children need to know that they can have an effect on bullies, not by fighting, but by being kind, even if only in thought.

> *How beautiful upon the mountains*
> *are the feet of the messenger*
> *who announces peace*
> *who brings good news*
>> (ISAIAH 52:7)

> *Thank you God*
> *For accepting us as your*
> *ambassadors of peace and good will*
> *Help us to encourage one another*
> *Amen*

PEACE IS POSSIBLE

In his farewell address to his disciples, Jesus promised, "peace I leave with you; my peace I give to you." (JOHN 14:27)

Does not the human heart long for peace within our own hearts, in our families and neighborhoods, in the whole world? And yet there is war, violence, injustice, oppression, everywhere on Earth. What will it take to bring about peace, lasting peace?

Pope Paul VI said that "if you want peace, work for justice." Mahatma Gandhi said that we must be the peace we wish to see in the world. Nelson Mandela, even after years in prison, was able to be positive as he worked to rid a divided South Africa of apartheid and have South Africa become a unified country. Many efforts are being made by groups internationally. The UN has designated September 21 as the annual International Day of Peace to commemorate and strengthen the ideals of peace both within and among all nations and peoples. It is hoped that this day could be a day of global ceasefire and nonviolence. Many groups observe this day for prayer for peace, including intercession for those who wage war.

The first Friday of October is dedicated to the annual Worldwide Children's Holy Hour of prayer for peace in our families and in the world. School children and parishioners gather at 11 am for this prayer, joining children from around the world who also gather in prayer for peace.

October 4 is the feast of St. Francis of Assisi on our church calendar. His prayer for peace is well known and sung in all our churches and faith gatherings: "Make me a channel of your peace." The words of the hymn are really a recipe for peace: Bring love to hatred, pardon to injury, faith to doubt, hope to despair, light to darkness and joy to sadness. Console others rather than seek to be consoled. Reach out to others with understanding rather than seeking to be understood. Forgive in order to be forgiven and love with all your soul. Let us all use this recipe in our own lives.

True peace is more than the absence of war and strife. It is about transforming our societies and uniting our global community to work together for peaceful and just solutions to conflicts. Each of us can and must do our part. *"Let there be peace on Earth and let it begin with me."* This is the opening line in a hymn by Jill Jackson-Sy Miller.

We must try to be the peace we wish to see in the world, that is, be a person of peace within our own hearts and in our relationships. We need to pray for peace as individuals and with groups, the peace that Jesus promises. Sincere prayer changes hearts; opens us to receive what we cannot achieve on our own. God gives to those who ask with humble hearts. Then we will become peacemakers, as individuals, families and communities.

Finally, we must work for justice. Much of the world's conflicts have injustice and oppression at the root. So we examine our own attitudes and behavior, and change what needs to be brought in line with the rules and ideals of justice.

Is peace possible? With God all is possible. Let us join the millions of peacemakers around the world and cooperate with God's plan for peace for all people. Yes, *peace is possible*. Let us pray with St. Francis...

Make me a channel of your peace

Amen

WAITING

Some time ago I spent much time in the waiting room of an intensive care unit of a hospital. The room was occupied by family members of critically ill loved ones, waiting for permission to visit, for words of hope and encouragement. This waiting time gave me the opportunity to reflect on the action of waiting.

"They also serve who only stand and wait." This saying is attributed to John Milton. So much of our time is spent in waiting: Waiting in line at the post office or in the grocery store, waiting in traffic, waiting for slowpokes to get ready. We are put on waiting lists for hip or knee replacements. We plant our gardens and seed our crops and then we wait for rain. We wait for the ripening of the harvest. Pregnant mothers wait for the birth of their babies. Parents wait for school to start again. Teens wait for their sixteenth birthday and their driver's licenses.

We know why we wait, what and for whom we wait. But how do we wait? In that intensive care waiting room I waited and watched others wait. I observed waiting with hope, waiting in tears, waiting in quiet desperation. I saw people chatting and teasing to lighten the mood. Others watched TV or did puzzles or tried to read to pass the time. I saw grandmas and daddy with a two-week-old baby waiting for word that his mommy would get better. I witnessed and experienced much pain, hope, compassion and shared tears. There was mutual caring and support of encouraging words and promise of prayer. The waiting was a religious experience of a loving God with loving people.

In this kind of setting it is understandable that the best in people is shared in the waiting. What about the other scenarios, the day to day and seasonal waiting? Is there a Christian response? When we pray for help for whatever need, do we tell God how and when to answer our prayer? Or do we have an attitude of patience and hope we find in Micah, "I will wait for the God of my salvation; my God will hear me." (MICAH 7:7) Sometimes we may feel that God is absent, hiding from us. Isaiah shows us how to respond. "I will wait for the Lord who is hiding his face...and I will hope in him." (ISAIAH 8:17) We can be assured that God always hears and answers us, but in God's time and choice of response which may not be the same as ours.

Back in that SICU room where my niece lay dying, I paraphrase John Milton's saying: "They also serve who only lie on their sickbed and wait." In the end, her prayer could have been, "I waited patiently for the Lord; he inclined to me and heard my cry." (PSALM 40:1) The sick and elderly in hospitals and nursing homes do indeed serve us and God by their example of patient suffering, by their attitude of prayerful presence before our God.

There is another one who waits. God waits for us when we wander away from him, waits for our response of love, waits to give us all that we need just for the asking in faith and trust. God longs and waits for our friendship. Let us pray with the psalmist:

Those who wait for the Lord shall renew their strength

they shall mount up with wings like eagles

they shall run and not grow weary

they shall walk and not faint.

(PSALM 40:31)

God does this and much more for us, his close friends
Let us not keep our God waiting
Praise and thanks to you, my God
Amen

ANNIVERSARIES

Anniversary celebrations abound in our lives: Birthdays, weddings, anniversaries of businesses, special personal achievements, remembrances of passing of loved ones and many other human events.

Why do we celebrate anniversaries and what is it that we celebrate?

An anniversary is the yearly remembrance of a significant event. The celebration keeps alive and deepens the significance of the original event. Authentic celebration remembers the past, rejoices in the present and looks in hope to the future.

Birthdays are the most common example. When I celebrate my birthday with family and friends I give praise and thanks to God who gave me the gift of life and who continues to sustain and bless this gift. Each year of life is precious. Birthdays give us the opportunity to be grateful for what has been, to rejoice in the present moment and to look forward in hope to continuing gift of grace from our loving Creator God.

Wedding anniversaries celebrate the faithful love of the couple for one another. In a real sense, anniversaries are more important that the wedding. I remember being at one of my niece's wedding. At the end of the ceremony the presiding priest addressed the gathered family and friends. He said something like this: "It is good that you have come to support and celebrate with this young couple. What is more important is that a year from now and every following year you remember to pray for them." It is indeed a remarkable milestone to reach 25, 50, 60 or more years of marriage.

With divorce rates as high as one in two or three, it is especially important to celebrate lasting marriages. It is also important that the community honour, celebrate and support these couples. Hopefully every anniversary, not just the multiples of five, is celebrated by all couples. A few weeks ago I saw an "older" couple get out of the car, he helping her, taking her arm protectively as they walked into church. I thought they must be married at least 50 years and still so much in love.

So I asked them. Their surprising answer was, "Four years!" Then I asked them if they celebrate their anniversaries. "Oh, yes, monthly. We're coming up to our 51st." Being quite certain that they wouldn't reach the significant 25 or 50 they decided on the monthly. "We celebrate in gratitude that God has brought us together. We are making new memories. Our relationship is so precious; every day could be a celebration. We are grateful for one another every day." It was an inspiration to visit with them.

Religious women and men also celebrate their faithfulness to their vowed commitment, thanking God for the blessing and unconditional love. As with wedding anniversaries, we need the participation and support of family, friends and the people we serve. I remember well what my priest uncle asked my home parish on the occasion of my 25th anniversary. He asked them if and why they wanted me to continue in my vocation and how they would support me. I have been supported for another 25 plus years and continue to be.

Whatever our vocation we make our commitment publicly before God and in the midst of the church. This takes place in community so that we are supported with prayer and presence. Our commitment is not only for us, the entire church relies on the witness of our faithfulness. At least once a year I renew my commitment "to live forever consecrated celibacy, gospel poverty and apostolic obedience."

At wedding anniversaries couples remember and renew their vows to be faithful till death. At each anniversary we are congratulated for making it to another milestone. We acknowledge that we could do this only by the grace of our faithful God and the support of family, friends and faith community.

Congratulations and may God bless you when you celebrate your special anniversaries!

THE POWER OF LOVE

Under the Earth's surface, faults and plates are shifting and rumbling causing earthquakes and aftershocks. The result is massive destruction, falling buildings, fires and floods and loss of life. Under the Earth's surface molten rock, magma is becoming restless, boiling, rising and eventually erupting with volcanic destruction.

One can use these images to describe what is happening in our world. Under the surface of daily life, there is anger seething in big cities, in countries with oppressive governments, in rich countries with an ever growing gap between the haves and have-nots.

Peaceful demonstrations for justice cannot remain peaceful if no one listens and nothing changes. The anger and frustration erupts into violence and destruction, revenge, vandalism, thefts, fires, disregard for the life and property of innocent people. And the crowds grow into uncontrolled and uncontrollable mobs, drawing youths looking for adventure into criminal activities.

We may ask, has our world's whole population gone mad? We can pray our feelings: How long will you people keep on destroying? How long will you love what is worthless and go after what is false? (See PSALM 4:2)

"Help, O Lord, for there is no longer anyone who is godly; the faithful have disappeared from humankind..." "Because the poor are despoiled, because the needy groan, I will now rise up," says the Lord. (PSALM 12:1 & 5) There is a proverb that says "More things are wrought by prayer than this world dreams of."

Surely we can't change what is happening in Libya, or Syria, or London, or even in Vancouver. Can we? Perhaps not, at least not noticeably. But we can contribute to the peace and harmony in our own hearts, families and community. When we get angry, (who doesn't at times) how do we respond? Anger is a feeling. We have the power to act with love and patience in any situation. We may not be feeling like loving. Though love is a feeling it is also a virtue. We can choose loving responses even when we feel anything but love.

St. Paul gives us the recipe for how to live as Christians, not just Christians, but all people, in 1CORINTHIANS: 13:4-8:

Love is patient and kind

It is not jealous or conceited or proud

Love is not ill-mannered, or selfish or irritable

Love does not keep a record of wrongs

Love is not happy with evil, but is happy with the truth

Love never gives up

Its faith, hope and patience never fail

Love is eternal

SETBACKS OR OPPORTUNITIES?

We experience various setbacks periodically throughout our life. Who of us has not suffered a setback in our efforts to lose weight? In our health? More painful is our failure in relationships. Financial setbacks impact more than ourselves. The most serious setbacks are spiritual, moral. These experiences can discourage us, tempt us to give up. "What's the use?" may be our response. Or they can be seen as opportunities. Our attitude makes all the difference.

We can learn from Saint Peter, that generous, boastful and yet humble disciple of Jesus. Oh, he had setbacks—the most serious kind. He was inspired to call Jesus the "Messiah, the Son of the living God." (Mt. 16:16) He was named the rock on which Jesus would build his church. Then came a setback. He tried to tell Jesus that he was mistaken about suffering crucifixion. This brought the most serious response from his Master: "Get behind me, Satan." Did this keep Peter down? Not at all. He was chosen to witness the transfiguration of Jesus on a high mountain.

Peter is remarkable in his ability to have setbacks and then to recover his usual self-assurance, even arrogance. He was bold enough to ask Jesus to invite him to walk on water. But then he chickened out and began to sink. (MATTHEW 14:28-33) As Jesus with his disciples left the last supper room, bold, arrogant Peter declared, "Though all become deserters because of you, I will never desert you." (MATTHEW 26:33) We know that it didn't take long before he denied even knowing Jesus, and this when his support was most needed.

Peter's story has good lessons for us in our own setbacks and failures. But it is not by looking at Peter, but by seeing how Jesus responds. No matter how often or how seriously Peter failed, Jesus continued to call him to be more than his failures, to be the contrite Peter who would make the triple declaration of his love for the risen Lord.

In our own setbacks, our failures, we, too, can turn to Jesus. He will forgive us, encourage us and strengthen us to continue on our journey. Even if we and others give up on us, Jesus will continue to believe in our goodness and give us what we need.

Give us this day our daily bread
Give us today all that we need to be our best selves
Amen

PARENTING WITH FAITH AND TRUST

Where did we go wrong? Were we too demanding? Not strict enough? Why have our children lost faith in all we taught them in word and example? These are agonizing questions I hear from parents. My own parents asked them. I remember one conversation I had with them saying something like this: "Do you know what you did for us? You taught us to think for ourselves. And now you find that some of us don't think as you do. And that is a gift you gave us. Now we take responsibility for our own decisions and actions."

I have met young parents who decided that they had religion thrust on them. They weren't going to do that to their children. So they give their children no experience of a faith community, having themselves abandoned the practice of going to church. I had a little girl in a grade seven class who was angry with her parents because, "they made me nothing. All the other kids are Catholic or Protestant, but I am nothing."

The parents thought that they had done her the favour of letting her choose. But what experience and background did she have to make a choice? They truly believed that they did what was right for their child. Now they have the opportunity to help her by giving her experiences of faith community, while also renewing their own faith.

Back to the question: Where did we go wrong? And an equally important question: What did we do right?

Let me give you some reassurance: *There are no parents who make no mistakes!*

I have heard a grandmother say, "We should be grandparents first. Then we would have the experience to parent." You do the best you know, what you believe is best for your children. You recognize what you could have done better. Also make sure you remember the good times when you did what was right. And this far surpasses the mistakes.

Once the children leave home and have children of their own, they make decisions based on their own experiences, their own circumstances, just as you did. That is now their responsibility. And they will do many things right and make some mistakes, too. As parent of the parents and grandparent of their children, your task is to love, support and pray. Most of all be thankful for God's trust in you by lending you children to raise for Him.

However the questions are good to ponder. If there is need to make amends to your children for what you did or didn't do, make amends. Ask for forgiveness and forgive yourself too. Having done so, move on, trust your children and trust God.

Prayer for Parents

God our Father, God our Mother
Teach us to be parents in your own parenting image
you said to your Son, you are my Son, in you I am well pleased
Help us to encourage our children by telling them we are well pleased
with them

Help us to know what to do when they fail

Help us to know how to make amends when we fail them and then to forgive ourselves

Finally, God, please give us the strength to let our children free trusting them the way you trust us

Amen

MANY KINDS OF STORMS

People may still be shocked by the devastation suffered in the storm Sandy, considered to be the worst storm in human memory. Every season brings its own storms, hurricanes, floods, earthquakes and cyclones. On our TV screens we see destruction of homes, public buildings and parks that now are piles of rubble. People die, power is interrupted for days, the numbers of homeless, cold and hungry people grows. We see people throw what were cherished possessions onto growing piles of rubbish. There are tears, courageous helpful acts and expressions of gratitude for lives that are saved.

These images are familiar images of what is happening in many parts of the world. We are reminded of what we, the human family, are doing in many parts of our Earth. Homes are destroyed, people are killed and displaced, and there are piles of rubbish that once were houses of worship, government buildings, stores and hotels. And thousands of refugees are fleeing to what they hope are safer places. We, humanity, are suffering in what seems to be an eternal storm of our own making. It is called WAR.

There was a time long ago when human beings became so corrupt that God regretted creating them. "The Lord saw that the wickedness of humankind was great on earth and it grieved him to his heart." (GENESIS 6:5-6) We know the story of Noah, the ark and the rainbow of promise. "I have set my bow in the clouds, it shall be a sign of the covenant between me and the earth. I will never again destroy every living creature as I have done" (GENESIS 8:21). As God looks down on our Earth now, does his heart regret his kindness to the human family?

We needn't look only to storms in other places. Let us look closer to home. Here, too, there is homelessness, hunger, destruction of property, the killing of people. We have found new ways to hurt one another with not just bullying, but with cyber bullying. We judge and misjudge others; families are torn apart through separations and divorce. There is growing greed for wealth and power. Our sins as the human family are many and grievous.

Does our loving God see our wickedness? Would he do to us what he did to the people in Noah's time? Would God honour the rainbow promise? No and yes. No, God will not destroy us. Yes, our God remains our loving creator. God sees our sins, yes; God also sees our repentance and goodness. His loving response is always a saving one, for God so loved the world that he gave his only Son, so that everyone who believes in him, may not perish, but may have eternal life. (JOHN 3:16) Jesus came, not to condemn, but to save.

As believing Christians, we enjoy the privilege of sharing in Christ's work of redemption. By every thought word and action we spread the goodness that Jesus came to bring. Let no one among us be made to feel less than others, no one left out of our smile, kind word and helping hand. Let us take to heart and try to live the Prayer of St. Francis:

Make me a channel of your peace!

Where there is hatred, let me bring your love

Where there is injury, your pardon, Lord

And where there is doubt, true faith in you

Amen

PART SIX:
DISCIPLESHIP

HOPE IN TODAY'S WORLD

Every newborn child is a sign that God continues to believe in the goodness of the human family, created in love, for love. Each child is God's hope for the world. Do you have hope in this world of ours? Every day in the news casts we hear of wars, bombs, rapes, poverty and destruction of all kinds. The state of our world may be enough to discourage the bravest heart. We may well ask with the psalmist, "Why are you cast down, O my soul, and why are you disquieted within me? Hope in God; for I shall again praise him, my help and my God." (PSALM 42:5)

If we, the adults, are discouraged and tempted to hopelessness, what must our young people feel about their future in this violent and mixed up world? What are their hopes for this world of ours? I asked the Grade 12 graduating class to share the hopes for the future. Their reflections certainly gave me hope. Here is what some of them said:

> "I hope that we will find better ways of living."

> "I believe everyone has potential to be good and do good."

> "I wish that all of us would accept differences in people, and that people would regain compassion, and realize that each and every person is an asset to the world, is important and needs to be valued and respected."

> "We can always have hope that things can and will get better."

> "We need to have people return to their religion and realize that without God we are lost."

> "I hope that we learn from the past and don't keep on repeating history, otherwise we will perish."

They hope and trust that eventually the world will become better, more peaceful.

What are the hopes of our young people for themselves? Further education and successful careers are important. They also desire happiness, love and family as well as freedom in their life choices.

> "I want us to make a difference in this world and to keep God in our life."

> "I hope I will be able to help people feel loved, respected and accepted."

They see hope as the best weapon against the unknown. They recognize that there is greatness inside all of them, and all it takes to let it out is someone to believe in them. People give hope. Above all they want to be the best people they can be.

The students acknowledge that they make stupid mistakes and try to learn from them. Some of the 'bad' things they do are because they are not mature enough to foresee the result of these actions. They don't want to be judged by their mistakes, nor by the behavior of others. They hope for understanding and guidance so that when they are the adults they will have learned from the experience of today's adults. They recognize that the worst actions in the world are mostly the actions of adults, of leaders.

> "When we are adults and leaders I hope that we will have learned from the mistakes of others as well as our own. We can make our world a better place to be."

Let us, the adults in the lives of these precious young people, give them all the love and support they long for and need. They are right when they say that every person needs to be valued, respected, accepted and loved. May every young person among us in our communities know how precious they are in our and God's eyes. They are our hope for a better future. And we thank God for them always.

Creator and Loving God

Hold these young people close to your heart

Help them to always remember your love for them

Amen

OUR HOME, PLANET EARTH

Home is where we live. We take care of it, keep it clean, beautify it. We take pride in how our house and yard look. Unity is our home town, Saskatchewan our province, Canada our country, Earth, our home planet. We can even go bigger. The Milky Way is our galaxy within the Virgo super-cluster of galaxies, in the universe. And all these levels of home are interconnected, interdependent. We are related to all there is. God has created and is sustaining all in life. God loves all of creation, the work of his hands, sees all as good. So how do we live in our home, Earth?

Our planet has been described as a body with the oceans, waterways and rain functioning as a circulatory system that provides life-giving blood, purifying and revitalizing the body (author Michael Dowd, *Earthspirit*). Water is an absolute necessity for the survival of all living beings. Yet the way we human beings have used and misused this precious gift creates the situation in which it is predicted that by 2025, two-thirds of the world's population will lack adequate supplies of fresh drinking water. Even today more than five million people die from water-borne diseases each year, 10 times the number killed in wars around the globe. These sobering statistics are provided by a member of the United Nations Non-Governmental Organization. Yes, water is a most precious gift of creation. No one understands this better than farmers whose livelihood depends on receiving enough in the form of rain at the right times. We have all endured thirst at some time in our lives and appreciate a cool drink on a hot day. Jesus promises to reward anyone who gives "a cup of water to drink to one of these little ones." (MATTHEW 10:42)

Water is an important symbol in Christian baptism, symbol of birthing, of washing, of new life in the Spirit of God. It is the sacred symbol of the Holy Spirit given as living water "gushing up to eternal life." (see JOHN 4:14) Water is an instrument of salvation related throughout Hebrew and Christian scriptures, from creation, to the flood, deliverance from slavery in Egypt, the baptism of Jesus, to name a few. It is within our power to save and renew it or continue to destroy it by our reckless wasteful use.

How are we to respond? What difference can each of us make? We can perhaps reduce the amount of water we use. The average amount of water used daily by each person varies from continent to continent: in North America, 150 gallons; in Great Britain, 88 gallons; in Asia, 23 gallons; in Africa, 12 gallons—barely enough to survive on. (UNNGO) We can urge governments to pass and enforce laws to greatly reduce the pollution of our rivers and lakes.

Most of all we can reverence and celebrate in gratitude the precious gift of water and all that our home, planet Earth, offers us. Let us also pray for wisdom, courage and motivation to follow through.

> *Creator God*
> *whose Spirit moved over the face of the waters*
> *who gathers the seas into their places and directs the courses of the rivers*
> *who sends rain upon Earth that it should bring forth life*
> *We praise you for the gift of water*
> *Create in us a sense of wonder and delight in this and all your gifts*

that we might receive them with gratitude
care for them with love, and generously share them with all your creatures
to the honour and glory of your name
Amen

GOD IN HAITI

The poor people of Haiti! As though it wasn't enough that they were already the poorest country in the Western Hemisphere; that they were underemployed and underpaid; that most of their produce was for export while their own children went hungry; that their governments have a history of corruption; that there were too many orphans and their cities were overcrowded, a most terrible event of a devastating earthquake struck them on February 19, 2010. Numerous damaging aftershocks went on for days.

Hundreds of thousands of people were killed. Many lost limbs, children were orphaned. Water, food and medicine were too slow in reaching the most desperate. Our television screens and newspapers showed us horrific images of suffering and devastation. We may well ask:

Where was God in all of Haiti's misery?

Speaking to Moses, God says, "I have observed the misery of my people who are in Egypt; I have heard their cry...I know their sufferings and I have come down to deliver them ...I will send you." Speaking to the world, God is saying, "I have observed the misery of my people who are in Haiti... I will send many to their aid."

And God fills the hearts of people all over the world with caring love. And the people, made in the image and likeness of God, respond. School children collect their pennies. Entertainers put on fundraising concerts. Red Cross, Doctors Without Borders and other charitable institutions rally to the needs of the earthquake victims.

And God gives wisdom and a spirit of generosity to governments of wealthier nations. Canada forgave Haiti its debt and urges other governments and financial institutions to do the same. The Canadian people opened their wallets to give generous donations, which are matched dollar for dollar by our equally generous government. Now leaders of many nations are considering how to help in rebuilding Haiti.

Yes, God is working miracles. Through the suffering of the poorest of the poor, people and nations are uniting in efforts to alleviate their suffering. God is acting in and through us, the many he sends. The stories of generous giving to those in need are stories of God's love for the poor. They are descriptions of how God calls on people to be his hands and heart. How privileged we are to be God's ambassadors.

Thank you, God, because you need us
May we be silent and open to hear your call
May we be loving and generous in responding to your call
May our united experience of this Haiti disaster be a constant reminder
that we are all your children brothers and sisters to all people
Amen

HARVEST TIME

September is harvest time. Combines, grain trucks and balers fill the air with sounds of promise. Garden produce is shared or preserved for the winter months. It is a time for rejoicing gratefully for good or bumper crops, or to express the perennial hope, "There is always next year."

Farmers and gardeners are not the only reapers and their earth-grown crops are not the only kind of crop. When Jesus saw the crowds he had compassion on them because they were harassed and helpless. Then he said to his disciples, "The harvest is plentiful, but the labourers are few; therefore ask the Lord of the harvest to send out labourers into his harvest." (MATTHEW 9:35-38) So when we pray for good crops and favourable harvest weather, let us also pray for the Lord of the harvest to send labourers into God's bountiful harvest. What is God's crop that is so bountiful? It is the people who feel lost, who long to hear the Good News that Jesus came to bring, people in our families and neighbourhoods.

Who qualifies to be recruited as a labourer in God's fields? All who are baptized and believe they have the Good News in their hearts to share with others. Yes, all of us are sent to share in the mission of Jesus Christ. God so loved the world that he gave his only Son to be the salvation of the world. Each person, baptized into the Body of Christ, is a recruit of the Lord of the harvest.

How do we go about this mission? No, we are not required to stand on street corners and preach about God's love. It is really quite simple. In our everyday lives we are given time and opportunity to proclaim the Good News. When we smile and greet someone on the street or in the post office or store, we are spreading joy. Visiting someone who is sick or lonely; affirming a child; remembering a birthday—these are a few ways of spreading God's love. Being honest and fair at work or play or school; treating others with respect as a child loved by God. You get the idea. In other words, it is living and relating with those around us as God intends his people to be and act.

Of course, praying for labourers often is interpreted as asking God to inspire more young people to answer the call to priesthood, to religious life, to be missionary. Certainly our church and world need more of the people who devote their lives totally to the mission of Christ, supporting the rest of us who live in families, raise children, teach or live daily lives of service while making a living. The key to being a good and faithful labourer in God's vineyard is to live our baptism, to continue growing and becoming the person our loving God created us to be. We walk in the divine presence with grateful and generous hearts. At the end, the Lord of the harvest will reward us beyond our imagining.

> *Let us pray*
> *for more of the special ministers in our lives*
> *Let us daily pray to be and become good recruits in God's harvest*
> *Lord, send labourers into your vineyard*
> *Send me*
> *Amen*

PART SEVEN:
CELEBRATING
SEASONS

SECTION 1:
JOURNEY THROUGH THE YEAR

THANKSGIVING REFLECTIONS

Each October we set aside a day during which we express our gratitude for the gifts we received throughout the year. We give thanks to our loving and generous God. We praise and thank God for harvests of field and garden, for the beauty and variety of creation with surprises that come with the seasons. We are grateful for sunsets and sunrises, for clouds and rainbows, for birds and flowers, for all that we enjoy on Mother Earth.

We thank God for family and friends, for the gift of life and time. We are grateful for freedom in our country and community, and for the intelligence and wisdom to choose rightly. Should we not also thank God's people who are God's hands and feet, heart and voice, making God visible in our lives? I name a few of the many to whom we owe thanks.

Thank you to all pastors who feed and strengthen our faith. Thanks to our faith communities in which we are at home, supported and loved.

Thanks to all moms and dads who by caring for and teaching their children are image of our Parent God teaching and caring for all his people.

Thank you, teachers in our schools, coaches of various sports, dances and figure skating—all that helps our youth grow and develop in wholesome ways as God intends.

Thank you doctors, nurses, home care-givers, volunteers—all who give of themselves so that we can live more healthy lives.

Thank you all seniors among us who share their wisdom and show us courage to accept and live through diminishment and pain.

Big thanks to civic leaders and labourers. You keep our community clear of snow and debris, and everything from water sewage and electricity in working order. And thanks, too, to our fire departments, and police, helping us feel safe.

Thanks to merchants, clerks, all the businesses that make the necessities of life locally available and do so with friendly smiles and cheery words.

Thanks to our newspaper personnel, the TV and radio staffs that keep us informed about local, provincial, national and world events.

There are others who deserve special thanks, too: caretakers of seniors' residences, schools and hospital, for example.

My hope is that when you read this, you will make an effort to thank anyone who is helpful to you and family.

> *God our Creator*
> *we thank you for your countless gifts and blessings*
> *May we learn generosity from you*
> *and share what we have with others*
> *that all may share in the gifts of your bounty*
> *Amen*

WISH LISTS

Pre-Christmas advertising presumes that people, especially children, will draw up lists of things they wish to receive under the tree. Retailers' wish list is that lots of people will buy lots of things. Letters to Santa, hints dropped at hopeful moments – the commercialism of Christmas forgets whose day it really is.

We have other wish lists that have nothing to do with getting stuff.

We wish for peace, in our homes and neighborhoods, our country, our world.

High on this list is healing and forgiveness, the deepening of relationships. We desire and hope that people suffering from natural disasters will receive the help they need, that there is caring in our world that no one is abandoned. We wish and pray for the end of human trafficking, the buying and selling of human beings, our sisters and brothers.

As part of our Advent preparation for the celebration of God's coming to live among us, we present our wish list to God who loves us unconditionally.

God has wish lists, too.

All God desires from us is to do justice, to love kindness and to walk humbly with God always present among us. (Micah 6:8)

God has plans for us, plans for our welfare and a future with hope. God desires us to call on him and promises to hear us. God wants us to search for him and promises to let us find him. (Jeremiah 29:11ff)

God loves us so much to desire that we share in his eternal life. God so loved the world that he gave us his only Son in Jesus born as one of us. And this so that we believe in him and have eternal life. (John 3:16)

Jesus affirms this: I came that you may have life and have it abundantly. (John 10:10)

We have so much to celebrate this Christmas and every Christmas to come.

As we gather with family and friends, let us do so gratefully. Let us also be mindful of those who have lost a family member this year.

As we gather with our faith community we give praise and thanks, as we receive our Saviour, the Bread of Life. And as we acknowledge the gifts we receive, may our wish list be something like God's own.

Let us welcome anew the Prince of Peace, Emmanuel, God with us

Come, Lord Jesus, come!

Amen

SUMMERTIME, FAMILY TIME

Schools are closed for the summer; students are busy about other joys: ball, swimming, camping— whatever families organize. And family reunions pop up everywhere. To be a family is a special gift of belonging designed by our loving Creator God. Our family gives us our identity. Besides sharing parents and grandparents we also share DNA, character traits, colour, values and faith. We grow up learning about relationships, the give and take of life. Our parents and siblings help to form us to be who we are. Belonging to a family is a special gift.

It is said that every family is dysfunctional in some ways. And being imperfect human beings, most of us contribute to our family's dysfunction. It seems in our nature to hurt the ones we love most. I suppose they are the safest ones to bear our anger. And then we learn to forgive and be forgiven. "A Christian's noblest victory is to forgive." (Blessed Theresa Gerhardinger, founder of SSND) We can learn from a grandmother who, when her brother was angry with her said, "I received his anger, wrapped it in love and returned it with joy." And his anger dissipated.

"Blessed" in the Catholic faith designates the first step toward canonization, or sainthood.

We all belong to another family, the family of God. When Jesus was speaking to the crowds, his mother and his brothers were waiting to speak to him. Jesus asked, "Who is my mother, who are my brothers?" and pointing to his disciples he said, "Here are my mother and my brothers. For whoever does the will of my Father in heaven is my brother and sister and mother." Indeed, Jesus considers each and all of us as his family, if we but do what God asks of us: to act justly, love tenderly, and walk humbly with our God. (Matthew 12:46-50)

Sometimes, unfortunately, members of families cut themselves off, imagining that they are sufficient unto themselves. Their family misses them and prays for their return. In the same way, some members of our Christian communities remove themselves from contact with those whose faith strengthens their own. Losing a sense of belonging could only result in loneliness, a feeling of having lost a part of who we are. In either case, forgiving and being forgiven will bring the wayward ones back to the fold. Then there is rejoicing that the lost has been found, as our Good Shepherd assures. (Luke 15:3-7)

This summer when we participate in family activities, let us be grateful for our families of origin and also our family of faith. Our sense of belonging is stronger when we participate in family and faith life. Summer holidays are not a dismissal from the faith family to which we belong. May summertime be family time in both of our families.

Loving God
praise and thanks to you for accepting us into your family
Amen

CANADA DAY – LET'S CELEBRATE!

Every year we celebrate Canada Day. Why? What do we celebrate? We have picnics and games and BBQs and fireworks. We wave flags and entertain one another and send balloons into the air. What does it all mean?

We rejoice and are grateful to be citizens in this beautiful, free, democratic land. We are a multicultural, freedom-loving people and are justly proud of our international reputation as peaceful, loving people. Is this still true of us?

Yes, we are each citizens of our country, our province and our town. We are also citizens of Planet Earth and the universe, related to all that is. Marshall McLuhan has said that "There are no passengers on Spaceship Earth. Everybody is crew." And as crew we all share responsibility for our Spaceship and one another.

But we are much more. Our citizenship is in heaven, and it is from there that we are expecting a Saviour, the Lord Jesus Christ. (Phil.3:20) We have been entrusted with the freedom of the children of God. Paul's letters describe the kind of freedom we are given as God's children, with some advice about living in this freedom.

Creation itself will be set free from its bondage to decay and will obtain the freedom of the glory of the children of God. (ROMANS 8:21)

Now the Lord is the Spirit, and where the Spirit of the Lord is, there is freedom. (2 CORINTHIANS 3:17)

For freedom Christ has set us free. (Galatians. 5:1)

For you were called to freedom, brothers and sisters, only do not use your freedom as an opportunity for self-indulgence. (GALATIANS 5:13)

And from 1 PETER 2:16: As servants of God, live as free people, yet do not use your freedom as a pretext for evil.

How are we, Christian Canadians, called to live in this freedom that is our gift from our loving God and preserved by responsible citizens? It is really quite simple. Each of us strives to make our corner of this wonderful land a better place for everyone, present and future. We take care of one another and the patch of Earth that is entrusted to us. We live gratefully.

Keeping our true citizenship in focus our celebration of Canada Day is an expression of our gratitude to God, to our ancestors, to fellow citizens, for all who make this land a wonderful place to call home.

> *God of the Universe*
> *look upon the people of this Canada of ours*
> *and bless us with peace, joy, harmony, generosity*
> *Bless the land and our homes*
> *May we always live in ways that are worthy of citizens of heaven and so*
> *rejoice your heart, O loving God*
> *In gratitude we pray in Jesus' name*
> *Amen*

LIVING GRATEFULLY

Every October we Canadians celebrate Thanksgiving Day. It is good to set aside a special day to remind us of our generous God's goodness to us. It is good to take time on that day to gather with family and friends, enjoy the fruits of God's creation and the work of our own hands and to offer prayers of thanksgiving. It is very good to gather every Sunday to offer thanksgiving with fellow parishioners. It is also very good to live gratefully every day.

When you give someone a gift, how can you tell if that person is grateful? *Thank you* may express gratitude, but could also be simple politeness. When a child receives a teddy bear or rag doll, hugs it, plays with it, sleeps with it, that child is grateful whether or not *thank you* was spoken. How do we show God that we are really grateful for the gifts so lavishly showered upon us? How do we treat the gifts of life, freedom, faith? How do we treat the gift of God's own Son, our Saviour? What about the gift of family and friends; of our beautiful planet home, Earth? We show our gratitude when we hug, play with, care for and love God's gifts to us.

What does day to day living gratefully look like, in my life, in family, in our community and country? I live gratefully by taking care of God's gifts to me, my own life by healthy living, by using my talents for the betterment of our world and the building up of the reign of God. I live gratefully for family, friends and neighbours by being loving and respectful to all among whom I live. I pray, "It was you who created my inmost self, and put me together in my mother's womb; for all these mysteries I thank you: for the wonder of myself, for the wonder of your works." (Psalm 139: 13&14)

As families and community we show gratitude by taking care of one another. It is a sign that our community is made up of grateful citizens when vandalism and littering just don't happen. There would only be cooperative efforts to make it a beautiful and pleasant environment for everyone. We are grateful citizens of our planet home, Earth, by making efforts to beautify our environment, by caring lovingly for all creatures: plants and animals as well as all people. Gratefully we avoid polluting and harming our Earth. Let us pray, "O Lord, how manifold are your works! In wisdom you have made them all; the earth is full of your creatures... I will sing to the Lord as long as I live; I will sing praise to my God while I have being." (Psalms 104:24 & 33)

Are we grateful Canadians? Are we grateful for the legacy passed on to us by the pioneers? Through their efforts we enjoy freedom to practice our faith, we have free education, good health care and a country of exceptional natural beauty and a democracy that gives each of us a say in how we are as a nation. Being grateful means taking responsibility for what we have. This includes taking time to become knowledgeable about issues and then take up our civic duty and privilege to vote. It is easy to take our privileges for granted.

Let us pray

Make a joyful noise to the Lord, all the Earth

Worship the Lord with gladness

Know that the Lord is God who made us

We are his people

Give thanks to him and bless his name

Amen

(Excerpts from Psalm 100)

FROM SEED TO HARVEST

Each fall so many gifts of fresh produce appear in homes for seniors: carrots, cucumbers, potatoes, tomatoes, corn, and such. Donors tend to remain anonymous. In May, just a few short months ago, these veggies were just seeds of promise. Then with careful gardening and favourable weather, voila! Full-grown veggies enough to share. Gratitude is the response to the generosity of the donors. Obviously the seed was good, the soil rich and rightly tended. The seed of promise produced a good harvest.

Jesus loved to tell parables of seeds and harvests. In each of the synoptic gospels he tells the story of the sower who went out to sow his seed. (Matthew 13:3ff, Mark 4:14ff, Luke 8:5ff) Jesus explains this parable. The seed is the Word of God, the Good News of salvation. The minds and hearts of listening people, our minds and hearts, are the soil that receives the seed. This seed is always full of possibility, good seed, only the best and most promising. What kind of harvest this seed will produce depends on how rich and fertile the soil of our minds, hearts and souls.

Perhaps I read the Word of God daily, and take it to heart. And every Sunday we hear the Word proclaimed and explained. I may decide to receive it as meant for me and mull over it so that I can make it part of my life. Or this is what I intend to do. Sometimes, by the time I get home to my everyday life, the busyness and distractions may have already taken it away, like the devil in the explained parable.

Or I listen to the Word and receive it with joy. It is just what I needed to hear to better my life. Then as the week progresses I am so taken up with all the happenings and distractions it may soon be forgotten, like the thorns that choke the life out of the sprouting seed.

I might be so happy to receive God's Word because it is exactly what I need at this time in my life. I am as careful to tend this seed as I am with my garden. I tend it with prayer, water and prune it with well-disciplined life, and fertilize it with deeds of kindness and sharing with others. When I fail and find a weed or two, I pull them out with acts of sorrow and asking for forgiveness.

The Sower, Jesus Christ, is the true Gardener of our souls. We are but his helpers, his servants of the Word to keep it growing and spreading like well-tended vines. We help it spread to our families, our neighbourhood, our town and beyond. When the harvest is ready at the end of our life, may it be a great harvest, the hundredfold that Jesus speaks about in his parable. Then may each of us hear the welcoming words: "Come, you are blessed by my Father, inherit the kingdom prepared for you."

Lord Jesus, divine gardener

you ask me to help tend the seeds and the tender shoots in your garden

May I not lose any of the precious seeds of your Word

With your grace may I gratefully receive your Word

tend it with careful hearing, water it with prayer

and share it with the people in my life

In the end may we enjoy a bountiful harvest of peace and love

in our families and community

Amen

HALLOWEEN – A FAITH MATTER?

Every October 31, our community is invaded with little, and not so little, ghosts and witches, pirates and princesses, maybe even little devils and angels. And goodies will fill their bags in response to their cries of "trick or treat." Why the 31st of October? When and how did all this start?

The origins date back about 2000 years with the Celts celebrating New Year's Day on November 1. They believed that ghosts of the dead returned on October 31 to roam the Earth. In the 7th century Pope Boniface IV designated November 1, All Saints Day, to honour saints and martyrs. The night before began to be called All-Hallows Eve and eventually Hallowe'en. Then around 1000 AD, November 2 was designated All Souls Day, a day to honour and pray for the dead.

Many of the ways we celebrate Halloween today are more pagan than Christian. But it doesn't have to be that way. I once had my grade one class dress as their patron or saint of their choice. We paraded all through the school telling about each of our saints. The school population and all the families learned much.

And who are saints? We know many that have been canonized in our church: Saints Peter, Paul, Theresa, Catherine, etc. There are also countless saints not so officially named, and not all of them are dead. Saints are those who live in God's love, with God's Spirit guiding and empowering them to show God's loving presence to others by word and action. There are several references to living saints in St. Paul's letters. He addresses his first letter to the Corinthians "to the church of God...to those who are sanctified in Christ Jesus, called to be saints." And in ROMANS 12:13 he exhorts his readers to "contribute to the needs of the saints and extend hospitality to strangers."

We are all called to be saints. We do this by living as Christ asks us to live, to love one another as he loves us, to forgive as we are forgiven, to act justly in all our dealings with one another and to pray and worship as a community of saints.

So let us enjoy the children on Halloween night, and if you plan one, have a great costume party. God loves his children, his saints, and wants them to have fun and enjoy life, as long as we also give joy to others.

Happy Halloween! Celebrate your feast day on November 1!

Then on November 2, pray for your beloved dead, and honour them as saints interceding for us as we continue our journey on the sainthood road. We believe in the communion of saints, those who have gone before us and those living among us.

All loving God and Father, our loved ones have died
They are gone from us into your light
We pray that you have forgiven them for any lack of love
and have welcomed them with open arms
into the joy and peace of your love
Be with us who miss them and grieve for them
Give us peace in the knowledge that we will be reunited
with all our loved ones when you call us to yourself
Amen

REMEMBRANCE DAY

Every November 11, we celebrate Remembrance Day. We remember in gratitude those who gave their lives for the peace and security. We keep recalling the brave fallen and the veterans who have survived, so that war would never again devastate our world. Yet wars continue to take lives and destroy lands. It causes me to wonder who remembers and what is remembered. Does the memory help leaders of nations find alternate ways of solving conflict and securing borders? Does this Remembrance Day help the world realize that wars just don't accomplish peace or security?

Every year we give prizes to children who enter poems or art into contests – to help them remember? Would it not be better to give them memories of the kind of efforts that bring real peace? PSALM 109 is a heart-rending prayer to have the memory of evildoers "cut off from the Earth." But "the memory of the righteous is a blessing." (PROVERBS 10:7) Let us hope and pray that our children, the future leaders, will grow up realizing that violence only breeds more violence. Help them learn and practice peaceful means of solving problems. November 11 is an ambiguous celebration of the gift of memory.

There are other remembrance days on our calendar. On December 25 we remember that "God so loved the world that he gave his only Son, so that everyone who believes in him may not perish but may have eternal life." (JOHN 3:16) In Holy Week and Easter we remember and celebrate the life, death and resurrection of the Son sent by God's love for us. Every time we gather for Eucharist we do what Christ asks: "Do this in remembrance of me." (LUKE 22:19)

In our own life we remember special events, special people, some positive, some we would rather forget. The faculty of memory is a wonderful gift. It helps us know who we are, where we come from. When we celebrate a past event, such as a birthday, we recall the gift of life, celebrate it in the present and look for continuing blessing in the future. It is precious gift to be able to remember.

God also remembers. Repeatedly in the Hebrew Scriptures God assures us the he remembers the covenant made to Abraham, Jacob, Noah and all the Earth. "He has remembered his steadfast love to the house of Israel." (PSALM 98:3)

And God forgets too. "I am the one who blots out your transgressions for my own sake, and I will not remember your sins." (ISAIAH 43:25)

If only we remembered God's unconditional love for each of us and for all people. How could one harm another who is so loved by the same God? If we did remember God's love, would not our world, our community, our homes and our hearts be at peace?

On November 11, when we gather to prayerfully remember our veterans and fallen loved ones, let us also remember our call as Christians to love as Christ has loved us.

Jesus, Prince of Peace, we pray for those from among us who died fighting for peace among nations

They have sacrificed their lives in the hope of making a difference in our world

May they now enjoy real peace, the peace only you can give

May their sacrifice not be for nothing

*Rather would leaders and decision makers in world nations come to
realize that there are other ways of achieving peace
May our nations stop sacrificing young men and women in hopeless battles
May each of us grow in our awareness and ability to live peaceful lives
within our homes, neighborhoods and countries
Grant eternal rest to the souls of our fallen heroes
Amen*

SECTION 2:
LENT

MARY SAID YES

On March 25, our Church calendar marks the event of the Annunciation of the angel Gabriel to Mary. It may seem incongruent to mark this event in the midst of the season of Lent when we centre our prayer and reflection on the passion and death of Jesus. But to me it is very appropriate. Mary's *yes* was not an easy one; nor one that would ensure her a place of honour among her own people. She was a teenage Jewish maiden, betrothed to Joseph though not yet living with him.

Now Gabriel tells her that God has chosen her to give birth to the Messiah, the very Son of God. Before she agreed she asked questions and stated her difficulty, discerning what this would mean for her. Once assured that it was God's will, she gave her response freely and unconditionally: "'Here I am, the servant of the Lord. Let it be with me according to your word." Through her, the will of God was turned into the body and blood of Jesus. (Joan Chittister, Order of St. Benedict, in *Lenten Reflections*) Because of Mary's *yes* at the Annunciation, we have Someone to journey with from desert through passion and death to glorious resurrection, Jesus, our Lord and Saviour.

> **Annunciation**
> The Christian celebration of the announcement by the Angel Gabriel to the Virgin Mary that she would conceive and become the mother of Jesus.

God chooses and speaks to us, too. We are also asked to discern our response. Christ asks us as he did Peter, James and John: "Could you not watch one hour with me? Watch and pray that you may not come into a time of trial." How will I keep watch with Jesus? Is it by making holy hours? Or is it to sit with Jesus in a sick, lonely or grieving person? Whatever the Word of God stirs in me, I am asked for a discerned response. May it be as free, humble and generous as was Mary's.

God is very creative in finding ways to reveal his will to us. The proclaimed Word in community worship is a powerful way. Scripture is God's revealed Word for us. We may not have the Angel Gabriel visit us, but parents, good friends and mentors are God's messengers, too. Women and men of wisdom with much life experience and deep faith are often there for us if we but open our minds and hearts to see and hear. Our conscience is a precious channel of God's will for us. It requires silence to hear this voice. It is in this silence within that we are able to discern God's will in every aspect of our daily life.

Our life is made up of daily decisions, some big and important, most just little ones that help us remain on the right path. Mary at the Annunciation and throughout her life, treasured and pondered God's Word. So may we ponder God's Word in life's daily events. When faced with a life-changing decision, may our discernment be true and our *yes* one of a servant of the Lord.

May Mary, humble maid of Nazareth, Mother of God's own Son, our redeemer, be our Lenten model for hearing and responding to God's will.

Holy Mary
mother of God and our mother
Pray for us

JESUS, FRIEND OF SINNERS

As we continue our journey through Lent, let us accompany Jesus as he walks the dusty roads of Palestine. Let us observe how Jesus relates to people others consider unworthy, sinners, like us.

"As Jesus was walking along, he saw a man called Matthew sitting at the tax booth and he said to him. 'Follow me.' And he got up and followed him. (MATTHEW 9:9) Being a tax collector, Matthew was hated by his fellow Jews. He was working for the oppressors, truly a great sinner. At Jesus' word, in his loving presence, Matthew experienced conversion of heart and became one of Jesus' closest friends.

As Jesus passed through Jericho, a crowd gathered to see this wonder-worker. Another despised tax collector, Zachaeus, also wanted to see. So he climbed a tree because he was too short to see over others. I suspect he may have had another reason to climb out of reach of those who disliked him. "Zachaeus, hurry and come down, for I must stay at your house today." The others grumbled because "he has gone to be a guest of one who is a sinner." Zachaeus welcomed Jesus with joy and also experienced conversion of heart. Jesus has that kind of effect on sinners who are open to his forgiveness and friendship. (LUKE 19:1 FF)

Jesus and his disciples had been walking the dusty roads too long in the hot sun. They came to Jacob's well in Samaria. Tired and hungry, Jesus sat by the well while his friends went into town to shop for groceries. Along came a Samaritan woman to draw water for her household's daily needs. It seems odd that she would come during the hottest time of day rather than in the cool morning when the other women surely had come. She knows that her neighbors look down on her and frown at her lifestyle. As she approached the well she noticed this stranger, a hated Jew, sitting there. What went through her mind? Did she consider going back home to return later. Did she mentally prepare herself for insults and perhaps even for physical abuse? We know what happened. As a result of a conversation with Jesus, experiencing his nonjudgmental, loving attitude toward her, this woman who had five husbands and was presently living with another man, this public sinner became an apostle to her own townspeople. (JOHN 4 FF)

After having the night with his Father on the Mount of Olives, Jesus came to the temple and found an angry, self-righteous crowd ready to stone a woman taken in the very act of committing adultery. Isn't it marvelous how the men who caught her missed the man with whom she was doing it? Perhaps here we see Jesus' compassion for the sinner at its best. He must have felt the injustice of dragging this woman to judgment while letting the man caught in the same act go free. He must have felt her shame in being exposed before all. And he saw into her heart as well as into the hearts of her accusers: Let the one without sin cast the first stone (JOHN 8:7). After all had slunk away, Jesus turned to the woman and asked: Has no one condemned you? Neither do I condemn you. Go your way and sin no more. Hopefully a few hearts besides this woman's experienced conversion that day.

There are many other examples in the gospels the depict Jesus as the special friend of sinners. Jesus said: I have come, not for the righteous, but for sinners. (MARK 2:17) I am a sinner, and that very fact entitles me to the special compassion and friendship of Jesus, risen Lord. He sees into our hearts and knows our weaknesses. He also knows our goodness and our growing love because we have been forgiven much and often. Jesus is our friend, ready to forgive as often as we turn to him, always loving us unconditionally.

Let us pray with the tax collector in the Temple:

God

be merciful to me, a sinner

Amen

LENT: A SPRINGTIME OF HOPE

Lent means spring and is a reminder that the season of new growing daylight and new hope for newness. Ash Wednesday is the beginning of Lent which leads us into the paschal events of the death and resurrection of Jesus. Our church asks us to observe Lent with prayer, fasting and almsgiving. It is an invitation to reflect on how we live our life as followers of Christ.

Prayer, spending quality time with God; fasting to become aware of our longing for God, almsgiving to care about others— three simple actions for our Lenten journey.

What is the call to fast? Physically fasting from food helps us to be in touch with other hungers, those for the things of God, for the gifts of the Spirit, for the all-loving presence of God. Fasting from food and other appetites may mean eating less, avoiding desserts, eating more simply. It may also mean watching less TV or giving up other activities that absorb too much of our time. Besides the physical benefits, fasting is a spiritual exercise. It differs from dieting to lose weight in its motivation. It will strengthen the will to follow the example of Jesus in the desert. His prayer and fasting strengthened him to withstand the temptations of the devil and prepared him for his mission. (LUKE 4)

Jesus was always concerned about the poor, helping and healing them at every opportunity. Almsgiving is one way in which we can follow his example. By our fasting we may save money that can be given to the needy. Giving money is the most obvious and probably easiest way to give alms. There are other ways. Time is a most precious commodity and may be just what someone needs from us. Sharing our talent, our special abilities, is another way to give alms. Almsgiving opens our minds and hearts to the needs and concerns of others and makes us more like Jesus.

Fasting deepens our longing for God which in turn leads to prayer. Prayer helps us realize that God also longs for us. During our Lenten journey we focus more and more on the events in Jesus' life that led to his passion, death and resurrection. We are encouraged to read Scripture more, participate in walking the Way of the Cross, and renew our personal and family prayer. Then we become more aware of, even amazed at, how great, how unconditional is God's love for us.

With prayer, fasting and almsgiving, our journey through Lent is a call to empty our lives of the trivial and superficial, to become aware of the important and lasting things that give meaning to our existence. Lent is a time of conversion, of starting over, of renewing our fervour. Most of all it is a time to walk in God's ever-present love toward its greatest outpouring in the Holy Week events. It is truly a springtime of hope.

Creator and loving God
help us to persevere in our Lenten efforts
to grow and become ever more like Jesus
Amen

HOLY WEEK – OUR PATH TO RESURRECTION

This is Holy Week, the week during which we annually remember and celebrate the life, death and resurrection of Jesus. These past weeks since Ash Wednesday, we have fasted, prayed more fervently, and given alms. Many of us have walked and prayed the Way of the Cross, remembering the great love and redemption our Saviour gave us. Nothing was too much for him. Yet he needed the support of his mother and friends who humanly helped him continue to the end.

What we are doing this Holy Week is more than remembering and reliving the past events of the first Holy Week some 2000 years ago. What gives real meaning to these celebrations is that they are still happening today. Jesus is still and always going through his passion and death in the sufferings of his sisters and brothers throughout the world and through the centuries, yes, including *our* suffering as we daily take up our cross and follow him. And as Jesus' own journey so long ago ended in resurrection, ours, too, will lead to new life in our risen Lord.

Way of the Cross

The journey of Jesus to the place of his crucifixion. Also a devotion consisting of prayers and meditations before each of 14 crosses or images set up in a church or along a path commemorating the events of the Passion of Jesus.

We have sung our hosannas in praise of our humble king riding a donkey. May we not join the fickle crowd that changed the song to the chant, "Crucify Him." Let us be aware that the successes of his followers are also his and continue our song of praise and thanks. We join him and his friends at the supper table on Holy Thursday sharing in the bread and wine that are the gift of himself inviting us to also be his body, giving ourselves freely and generously. As we allow our king to wash our feet, let us also be willing to serve one another, especially the neediest among us. Let us join him and Peter, James and John in his struggle in the garden. As he pleads with these three chosen disciples, he pleads with us in the suffering people around us: "I am deeply grieved, even to death. Remain here and stay awake with me." We join his prayer, "My Father, if it is possible, let this cup pass from me; yet not my will but your will." (Matthew 26:38-39)

What is there to say on Good Friday? Let us follow him silently, sorrowfully, accompanying Mary, John, Mary Magdalene and the other faithful women as he makes his painful way to his death on the cross. We hear him say, "Father forgive them, they don't know what they are doing." We search our own hearts for any refusal to forgive others and pray to be able to join Jesus' act of forgiveness. Then we will also be forgiven, for we too have no idea of the many ways we hurt others in word, action or neglect.

As we venerate the cross by genuflecting, touching or kissing it, symbol of our salvation, let us pray for the people, our sisters and brothers in our families, community and around the globe who are unjustly condemned and 'crucified' by the injustice in our own hearts and in our world.

Holy Saturday is a day of waiting. After Jesus was laid in the tomb and it was secured, Mary Magdalene and the other Mary were there, sitting opposite the tomb. (Mt. 27:61)

In the evening we begin to celebrate the resurrection at the Easter vigil, the most joyous of all celebrations! This is the promise of our own resurrection! This is what gives us hope throughout our lives. Jesus was obedient to the point of death, death on the cross. Therefore God has exalted him. (Philippians 2: 8-9) In his victory over death is the promise of our eternal life with our risen Lord. Alleluia!

Lord Jesus
may your death on the cross and resurrection into new life
be a source of encouragement and hope to all
who are unjustly condemned
May we be encouraged and strengthened to work for peace
The peace you died and rose
to bring to all who believe
Amen

SECTION 3:
EASTER

EASTER PEOPLE

We are Easter People, and Alleluia is our song!

I remember when this was a popular slogan, I believe in the '70s. One could see it on posters and even on bumper stickers.

Yes, we are Easter People. Jesus, our risen saviour is alive and among us. We share his risen life. During this 50-day Easter season let us prayerfully examine the resurrection scripture stories and reflect on how we are called to live the values and joy of risen life.

Easter people are apostles and evangelizers. We share the good news of new life, a new way of being community. Jesus says to Mary Magdalene and the other Mary, "Go and tell my brothers..."and to the disciples, "Go, make disciples of all nations..." (MATTHEW 28)

We do this by word and way of life, teaching our children and witnessing to friends and neighbors.

We look for the risen Lord among the living, that is, within our community. "Why do you look for the living among the dead?"(LUKE 24:5) The community of believers is united and the members take care of one another so that there is "not a needy person among them." (ACTS 4:34)

We are a people of peace and forgiveness. Jesus meets his disciples in their fear-locked state and greets them, "Peace be with you." Then he breathes the Holy Spirit on them and commissions them to be forgiving and forgiven people. That is how we become people of peace, to forgive one another and never hold grudges. Jesus has given us his Spirit, his power to do so. (JOHN 20:19-23)

Easter people are people of hospitality and table fellowship. "As they came near the village to which they were going...they urged him strongly, 'stay with us because it is almost evening and the day is now nearly over.' So he went in to stay with them." We remember how these disciples recognized him in the breaking of the bread. Each time we break bread together do we recognize the risen presence among us? (LUKE 24:28FF)

When we have a barbecue in the back yard or at the lake, we could be mindful of the one the risen Jesus hosted for his fishermen friends. When they had gone ashore they saw a charcoal fire there with fish on it and bread. "Come and have breakfast," is Jesus' invitation. (JOHN 21:9FF) He invites us also to come and share the bread of Word and communion on Sunday mornings.

When we live the risen life we love much, no matter how many times we fail. Peter learned this when, after the barbecue breakfast, Jesus asked him how much he loved him. His failures did not cause him to be distrusted. No, "Feed my lambs; feed my sheep." We are loved unconditionally. Therefore we can love much. "If we love one another, God lives in us, and his love is perfected in us." (1 JOHN 4:12)

As Easter People our everyday lives, all our actions, are manifestations of the risen life. The resurrection of Jesus has changed history forever. We can no longer be the same since we share his life by our faith and baptism. What peace and love and joy are ours!

We are indeed Easter People and Alleluia is our song. May we never forget its tune.

> *Risen Lord Jesus*
> *reign in our hearts and in our community*
> *May we be good witnesses of your risen presence among us*
> *Amen*

THE SPIRIT IS A-MOVIN'

The Spirit is a-movin' all over, all over this land. This 1969 Carey Landry Pentecost hymn celebrates the empowering and all-pervasive presence of God's Spirit in, among and beyond us. Pentecost Sunday, is the day we remember the tremendous outpouring of the Spirit on the gathered community. (ACTS 2) This was not the first coming of the Spirit. Throughout the old and new testaments there are accounts of people and events enlivened by this same Spirit. The Spirit is also described as Holy Wisdom, the Breath of God, the wind of God, the gentle breeze in which Elijah recognized God's presence. (1KINGS 19:13)

God's Spirit hovered over the chaotic waters when earth was but a formless void. (GENESIS 1:2) God had "formed man from the dust of the ground and breathed into his nostrils the breath of life. This is not unlike what the risen Jesus did when he breathed on his disciples and said, "Receive the Holy Spirit." (JOHN 20:22)

Among the many Old Testament people who were filled with the Spirit of God we find Bezalel called by God who "filled him with divine spirit;" David, who was anointed in the presence of his brothers, and the spirit of the Lord came mightily upon him from that day forward; Jephthah, for "the spirit of the Lord came upon him." If you have ever watched the program *Twice in a Lifetime*, you must have wondered if Othniel, the judge, was for real. Just check JUDGES 3:10 and you will learn that "the spirit of the Lord came upon him and he judged Israel." In ZECHARIAH 7:12 we read that the people refused to believe "the words that the Lord of hosts had sent by his spirit through the prophets."

ISAIAH 11:2 describes how a descendent of David will receive the spirit, "The spirit of the Lord shall rest on him." At Jesus' baptism this is fulfilled: "And a voice came from heaven, 'you are my Son, the Beloved; with you I am well pleased'." (LUKE 3:21-22) Then, Jesus, full of the Holy Spirit, returned from the Jordan and was led by the Spirit in the wilderness.

These few examples are enough to show us how present the Holy Spirit has been from the beginning of time and throughout history. But just in case we still do not get it, God gave us this very spectacular and powerful manifestation at Pentecost.

Surely on that day Peter and all the others were filled with the Holy Spirit speaking now without fear in ways that all understood. That same Spirit is with each of us and with all of creation. At our baptism and confirmation we celebrate again this spiritual power given to us.

How is the presence of this Spirit manifest among us? When we live in love, joy, peace, patience, kindness, generosity, faithfulness, gentleness and self-control. These are the fruits of the Spirit as listed in GALATIANS 5:22-23. We are empowered to live this way by the Gifts of the Spirit: the spirit of wisdom, understanding, council and might, knowledge and fear of the Lord. (ISAIAH 11:2-3) These gifts and fruits are given to individuals and communities. May we encourage one another to believe in God's outpouring of the Spirit within each of us, among us and indeed in the whole created universe. Listen to the News, look around with the intention to see signs of the work of the Spirit: SAVE THE CHILDREN and THE RIGHT TO PLAY movements; neighbors helping neighbors; nations striving to eradicate poverty; you get the idea.

Yes, the Spirit is a-movin' all over this land.

Come, Holy Spirit
Fill our hears with love and joy
Amen

GO TELL …

Over and over Jesus commissions his followers to go tell.

To Mary Magdalene and the other Mary, "Go and tell my brothers to go to Galilee; there they will see me." (MATTHEW 28:10)

In JOHN 20:17 to Mary Magdalene, "Go to my brothers…" The angel in the tomb to the women who came to anoint the body of Jesus, "… Go tell his disciples and Peter that he is going ahead of you to Galilee…" (MARK 16:7)

To the gathered disciples, "Go into all the world and proclaim the Good News." (MARK 16:15 also MATTHEW 28:19)

There is a sense of urgency in these commissions. The Good News of the resurrection must be told everywhere. Once we hear and believe it, we are impelled to share it, like the two disciples from Emmaus. How discouraged and downhearted they were before they knew that Jesus was alive. Once they recognized the truth they just had to go back to Jerusalem and tell the others. So it must be with us. We know and experience the presence of our risen Lord and Saviour. We must share it with others.

How do we do this in daily life? Few of us are sent to the ends of the Earth as missionaries to spread the Good News of salvation in foreign lands. No, most of us are sent into our own homes, workplaces and neighbourhoods. Jesus gave us precedence of this. After he was freed from the demons that possessed and tortured him, the man begged Jesus to let him follow him. But Jesus refused saying, "Go home to your friends and tell them how much the Lord has done for you." (MARK 5:19) To be disciples who go and tell in our daily lives we live as resurrection people, filled with the Holy Spirit.

Resurrection people have a positive outlook on life with all its ups and downs. They spread joy wherever they are. Even in the midst of trials like sickness, death of a loved one, loss of any kind, they have grateful hearts. When news is of violence and disasters of all kinds, Easter people find hope and bring concerns to prayer. They are not afraid to love, even after they have been rejected. They believe they and others are loveable and loved, even when their actions are not loving. Easter people know that forgiveness and love are unconditional from our God who is love. They do not repeat negative words about others, avoiding all gossip that can be so harmful.

Yes, Jesus sends us as he sent his disciples, to go and tell his message of peace, love and salvation for all. His message is to love one another as he has loved us. It is to follow his example of humble service, to empower people rather than overpower them.

Let us listen in our hearts and hear the words, "Go, tell everyone that I am with you, within you, till the end of time. Then come and share my eternal home forever.

Jesus Christ is risen! Alleluia!

BE THE STONE?

Years ago in a parish where I was serving, I gathered a group of eight to 10-year-old children to reflect with them on the Resurrection. We told the whole story: Jesus in the tomb guarded by soldiers; the big stone sealing the tomb so the disciples couldn't steal the body and say that Jesus had risen; the women looking for Jesus' body to do more embalming; the angels asking why they are looking for the living among the dead. I had the children reflect on the scene and asked, "If you were there, what would you do? Who would you be? Some wanted to be like the women looking for Jesus. Some even wanted to be Jesus to experience coming alive again. But the choice of one little boy has stayed with me over the years.

"I would want to be the stone." The big stone that closed Jesus' tomb? Why?

"I would let Jesus out!" His childish theology didn't give him the insight that nothing could hold Jesus back. Neither stone nor wall could keep the risen body of Jesus from going where he wanted to be. Only a stone of my making can keep Jesus in, or out. Every year I reflect on being the stone.

One of Jesus' favourite dwelling places is our heart, but he will not enter without our opening the door. His respect for our God-given freedom is too great. "Listen, I am standing at the door, knocking; if you hear my voice and open the door, I will come in and share a meal. (Rev. 3:20) We open the door by being welcoming to others, especially the poor, the sick, the lonely. This would be like the stone that lets Jesus in.

Is it possible to be the stone that keeps Jesus from coming out? We have this wonderful treasure of our faith. We believe Jesus' words, "Those who love me will keep my word, and my Father will love them, and we will come to them and make our home with them." (John 14: 23) We keep this special treasure, this Good News to ourselves when we avoid speaking about our faith. Maybe we are too shy or too afraid that others will think I am too holy, believing myself better than others. These days I often hear people say, "Never talk about religion or politics, especially with family and friends." But, just before ascending to the Father Jesus gives this strong commission to his followers: All authority in heaven and on earth has been given to me. Go therefore and make disciples of all nations, baptizing them in the name of the Father and of the Son and of the Holy Spirit, and teaching them to obey everything that I have commanded you. And remember, I am with you always, to the end of the age. (Matthew 28:18-19) We are today's disciples receiving this mission.

One other way of being stone, or rather having one is from Ezekiel 11:19.

I will give them one heart, and put a new spirit within them. I will remove their heart of stone from their flesh, and give them a heart of flesh.

At the scene of Resurrection, what will you do? Who will you be? Hopefully all of us will be believers filled with joy that Christ is risen indeed and will be with us always!

Let us sing
Jesus Christ is risen today
Our triumphant holy day
who did once upon the cross, suffer to redeem our loss
ALLELUIA! ALLELUIA! ALLELUIA!

DINING WITH THE RISEN CHRIST

Shared meals strengthen family unity and build community. They are the mark of hospitality. With a meal we celebrate special events, birthdays, weddings, anniversaries, Roughrider success. Meals can become simply the need for nourishment, or they can be a sacred event.

The gospels have numerous stories indicating the love Jesus had for sharing meals. He loved to eat with anyone who invited him. He had a standing invitation in Martha's house which was his home away from home. (LUKE 10:38) Jesus accepted an invitation to a wedding at Cana and provided much wine for the celebration. (JOHN 2) Simon the Pharisee invited him without offering the customary hospitality rituals of foot washing and anointing with perfume. This unfriendliness did not deter Jesus from sharing his table and while there, he accepted the ministrations of penitence and love from a sinful woman. In fact, Jesus gave preference to publicans, tax collectors and sinners because, he said, "I have come, not to call the righteous, but sinners." (MARK 2:17) Jesus was criticized for eating with them at Matthew's invitation and he even invited himself to Zacchaeus' house.

Jesus also hosted meals. When he was concerned for the crowd who had been with him all day he provided food for their journey back home. These occasions were like outdoor picnics at the end of a day of listening to Jesus' message of salvation. He gave an example of saying grace before eating: "He looked up to heaven and blessed and broke the loaves." (MATTHEW 14:19)

After his resurrection, Jesus met two dejected disciples on the way to Emmaus, accepted their invitation to stay with them and blessed and broke bread with them. He also hosted a BBQ on the seashore. When the disciples came ashore with their miraculous catch of fish "they saw a charcoal fire with fish on it and bread." JOHN 21:9)

The Passover supper he hosted the night before he died was the greatest meal of all. Now our risen Saviour invites us to this sacred meal, the Eucharist, where he is both host and food for our faith journey toward the kingdom of God, often describe as a wedding banquet

These reflections lead us to remember to invite the risen Christ to our table whenever we gather, and to follow his example of saying grace. We could use the traditional one:

Bless us O Lord and these thy gifts which we are about to receive from thy bounty, through Christ our Lord.

Or we could be more creative...

Risen Lord
Bless those who have grown this food with their hands
those have prepared it for our nourishment
May we be generous to those who have less than they need
May we remember your presence among us as we share this meal
Amen

PEACE, THE GIFT OF EASTER

"Father, forgive them, they know not what they do." This was Jesus' dying prayer to his Father. Who all is included in the ones who don't know what they are doing? The soldiers who so badly mistreated him and pounded nails through his hands and feet; the leaders of his own people and the crowd who shouted "Crucify him;" the weakling Pilate who thought washing his hands would exonerate him; Peter who denied him; Judas who betrayed him; all those who deserted him. Yes, Jesus asked God that all these be forgiven as he had already done.

That is not all. Jesus looked down the corridors of time to centuries past, and those yet to come. He saw the sins of all, yes, my sins and your sins, asking the Father to forgive us because we don't know what we are doing. It is for this that the Son of God, son of Mary, lived among us, teaching us and dying for us, for "God so loved the world that he gave his only Son, so that everyone who believes in him may not perish but may have eternal life." (JOHN 3:16) It is for this that Jesus died and rose on the third day.

After his resurrection from the dead, he visited his disciples, his friends, with the greeting, "Peace be with you." And Jesus said to them again, "Peace be with you. As the Father has sent me, so I send you." He then breathed on them saying, "Receive the Holy Spirit. If you forgive the sins of any, they are forgiven. If you retain the sins of any, they are retained." (JOHN 20:20-23)

Now we, his disciples and friends, are sent to carry the gift of forgiveness into our life and in our relationships. Who of us has not been sinned against by people close to us? And who of us has not sinned against others? Let us learn from Jesus to forgive and pray, "Father forgive them, forgive me, for we do not know what we are doing." Then in our hearts the words of our risen Saviour ring clearly: "Peace be with you."

The Gift of Easter is the peace that comes with forgiveness. When we forgive we give peace, when we are forgiven we experience peace, the kind of peace Jesus died for. His peace is not like that of the world, it is the peace that comes from being in union with our triune God. (JOHN 14:27) No one can take this peace from us. Only when we lack trust in Jesus' promise of Peace, when we forget how loved and forgiven we are, only then would we experience the loss of this Easter Peace.

Jesus stood in the midst of his disciples and said to them "Peace be with you!" Jesus also stands in the midst of us whenever we gather. May we let his words resound in our hearts and be grateful that God loved the world so much that he gave his Son to be our Saviour, our brother, our teacher. Let our glad alleluias ring out our joy and gratitude.

Peace be with you

PART EIGHT:
OUR FAITH JOURNEY

CELEBRATING ADVENT

The season of Advent begins four weeks before Christmas. As Christians we live in the faith context of longing for a renewed experience of salvation because, "God so loved the world that God gave his only Son, so that everyone who believes in him will have eternal life." Our church urges us to live Advent as a time to refocus our attention to the reason Jesus was born, to realign our lives and wait for him to come again.

We also live in secular society which uses this time to maximize profits, to con us into expensive gift giving, to celebrate "the holidays" without mention of its original reason. Is it possible to live in both the world of faith and the world of consumerism? As Christians are we expected to opt out of secular celebrations and practices in order to be true to the purpose of this joyful season of Advent?

I believe there are ways to reconcile the two without losing sight of the One whom we celebrate. Christmas lights can be a symbol of the coming of Christ, the light of the world. Each evening when we turn them on why not accompany this action with an invocation, such as "Come, Lord Jesus, be light in our lives, our community, our world."

The Christmas tree can be a reminder that Jesus' coming for our salvation resulted in his death on the tree of the cross or be a symbol of Jesus the vine and we the branches. Decorations on the tree and within the home tell us that someone very important is coming and has come into our midst. Christmas baking can remind us that Jesus is bread for the world, that he fed thousands of people, and that he loved to join people for meals. Let us not forget to invite this honoured guest to our Christmas dinner.

Gift giving is symbolic of the greatest gift of all, Jesus, given for our salvation. Reflecting on the great gap between the haves and have-nots in our world may inspire us to give to someone needy instead of overwhelming one another with heaps of unneeded things. Whatever we give to the least we give to Jesus whose birthday it is that we celebrate.

It may be helpful to space out the decorating, adding the last finishing touches a day or two before Christmas and so give a sense of waiting. Waiting is not a popular activity in our society, but it is a good practice in patience and can have a calming effect on us. When we find ourselves waiting in lines, we could take the time to reflect on the coming of the Prince of Peace and ask that peace come into our hearts, our families, and our world. And let us not forget the traditional advent practices, the advent wreath, the Jesse Tree, an advent calendar. All these help to put us into a spirit of waiting, of getting ready for something great.

Finally, let us not ignore the invitation to celebrate Jesus' birth, but join all believers at his great party in church on Christmas day. It is, after all, his birthday.

> *Joy to the world!*
> *The Lord has come into our midst*
> *May our hearts be ready to receive you*
> *Come, Lord Jesus*
> *Amen*

COME, LORD JESUS!

"See, I am coming soon... I am the Alpha and the Omega, the first and the last, the beginning and the end... Surely I am coming soon. Amen. Come, Lord Jesus!" (REVELATIONS 22:12, 13, 20)

Who is it that we want to have come? It isn't the infant Jesus born in Bethlehem more than 2000 years ago. He lived among us, taught us wonderful Truths about how to live fully human lives, and showed us the Way to eternal life with God. He died on the cross for us, was buried and is risen. Now he is always with us, until the end of the world. So who is it we wish to have come? Can Jesus come again and again? We know he will come at the end of time; but what about now? Today?

Are we concerned about the many wars on our earth? The killing of innocents, the genocides? What about domestic disputes, the hatred and violence in the streets of our cities? What about the struggles, the mini wars in our own hearts?

Then let us pray: Come Lord Jesus, Prince of Peace!

Are we concerned about the hungry and starving of our world? Do we experience spiritual hunger, emptiness in our lives?

Let us pray: Come, Lord Jesus, Bread of Life!

There is so much darkness of ignorance that leads to misdirected violence; ignorance of what is of true value, ignorance about others who are different, and so not worthy of respect.

Let us pray: Come Lord Jesus, Light of the World!

So many people, especially women and children, suffer under male domination, in governments, in misunderstood religion, in the slavery of the sex trade.

Let us pray: Come Lord Jesus, Good Shepherd!

Are we burdened with sin, our own and the sins of society?

Let us pray: Come Lord Jesus, Lamb of God, who takes away the sins of the world!

Are we or our loved ones sick, crippled, addicted, despairing, and sorrowing?

Let us pray: Come Lord Jesus, Divine Healer!

Yes, Jesus can and does come again and again, as often as we open our hearts in humble need. This Christmas let us joyfully and gratefully celebrate the unconditional LOVE of our God who loves us so much that he sends his only Son to be our Saviour in every situation of our lives.

Come, Lord Jesus
come into our hearts, our families, our community,
our country, our world!
Amen
Come, Lord Jesus!

ADVENT, A TIME OF WAITING

We have begun our Advent journey and are waiting. For what and for whom do we wait? We wait and prepare for our annual celebration of the coming of the Son of God, son of Mary, born one of us in Bethlehem so long ago. We also wait for the Lord of the Universe to come at the end of time 'to judge the living and the dead,' as we pray in our creed. In the meantime, Jesus Christ, risen Lord and God, comes to us in many ways throughout our lives: in the celebration of Eucharist, in people who love us or need us, whenever we open our minds and hearts to be with him in prayer and in being like him in our love for one another.

Many who wait may not be aware that it is for the Saviour, Jesus Christ. Some wait for food as they languish in starvation environments. Others long for a place to call home. Many women, children, minorities, wait for equality, for justice. I rejoice that after 28 years of struggle for justice, female postal workers are finally being paid the same salaries as their male counterparts. Canada Post is required to give 28 years of back pay with interest. Almost daily we hear and read news of abuse of women, young girls and little children. In our own country as well as in Afghanistan and other oppressive nations, all who are oppressed cry out for justice. Yes, they long for a Saviour who has come and who continues to come with the help of faithful followers.

Let us look within our own community, our schools and sports arenas, and our homes. Is there among us someone who is being bullied, ignored, or treated badly? The jingle we used to say, "Sticks and stones may break my bones, but words/names will never hurt me" just isn't true. The fact is, name calling, put downs, and harsh judgments do hurt, cut deeply and cry for healing.

Do we wait for our Saviour, today, tomorrow and celebrate his coming at Christmas? All of us who were ever hurt and/or have hurt someone else, wait for forgiveness and healing, for peace among us and in our world. We prepare for the coming of our Saviour and celebrate with Christmas joy!

During this Advent time let us open wide our hearts and minds as we pray:

Come, Lord Jesus, save us!
And God says, "My people, I wait for you to open your hearts
to receive my greatest gift, my only Son
I sent him so that everyone who believes in him
may not perish but may have eternal life
I so desire for you to accept Jesus as your redeemer and friend
Follow his teaching and imitate his example of love and gentleness
Love one another, forgive one another
and you will find peace, harmony and eternal happiness"
Amen

ADVENT PEOPLE

Advent people are those who wait and help us wait for salvation, the redeemer sent by our Creator God. The prophets of old are such people, especially Isaiah who promises times of peace and plenty when HE comes. These will be times when the wild animals get along and are safe for children to play among them. They are times when God will provide tables laden with rich food and good wine. (Isaiah 25:6) The last of the prophets, John the Baptist, is an Advent person who cries out in the wilderness "proclaiming a baptism of repentance for the forgiveness of sin..." (Luke 3:3 ff)

Mary, Joseph and Elizabeth are intimately woven into the Advent-Christmas events. They have heard and taken to heart the messages of the prophets concerning God's plan to send a Saviour. They were ready to believe the unbelievable, to become part of the story of salvation. We can learn from them how to be Advent people.

Can you imagine how hard it was for Mary, that humble maid of Nazareth, to believe and say yes to what God asked of her? In Luke's account we see how she questioned and discerned whether this request to be mother of God's Son was truly God's will for her. Humbly she acquiesced to this unbelievable request. In saying yes she realized that becoming pregnant before she and Joseph lived together was putting her in danger of being stoned. But, believing this truly was God's will, she trusted that God would bring this event to completion, she knew not how.

Joseph, too, struggled to accept this mystery. In taking the pregnant Mary into his home, he would also be in danger from the strict observance of the Mosaic Law. Mary's cousin, Elizabeth, is also an Advent person as is her husband Zachariah. Elizabeth's heart was so attuned to God's presence that she readily recognized that Mary was coming as "God-bearer." She praises Mary for her faith: "Blessed is she who believed that there would be a fulfillment of what was spoken to her by the Lord." (Luke 1:45)

How do we discern God's will for us this Advent season and beyond? Are we able to hear the voice crying in the wilderness of our hearts, calling us to repentance and forgiveness of sin? Is it possible that God is asking something special of us? John challenges people to share clothing and food with those who have less. (See Luke3:11) And Mary's song of praise is a masterpiece of social justice. (Luke 1:46-55)

Maranatha
Aramaic Advent word for "The Lord Comes."

As Advent people we respond to the call to share through Secret Santa so that food hampers and gifts can be delivered to the needy in our own community. All year our food bank and New-to-You store are available to all in need. Perhaps we are called to change our social system. In our country and our world all is not right and just if some people have little opportunity to earn an adequate living while others amass millions and billions more than they will ever use. What would the Baptist cry out in our world today? Maybe, just maybe, some of us are called to be that voice.

Let us pray to our Advent Mentors...

John, Mary, Joseph and Elizabeth
Show us the way
MARANATHA!
COME LORD JESUS!
Amen

ARE YOU HUNGRY?

Are you hungry? According to the UN Food and Agriculture organization, more than one billion people suffering from malnutrition would respond, "Yes." Statistics tell us that one child dies every six seconds because of malnutrition. Consulting the Internet I learned that 104,414 Canadians turn to food banks monthly to help them get by. How many in our own community need the help of donated food? World leaders gather in world summits on food security. So far they have been unable to arrive at solutions that would create food equity for all people. So the hunger, and starvation continue.

Are you hungry? My answer is and always has been, "No, I always have enough daily nourishment." But there are other kinds of hunger and thirst. The words, *hunger* and *thirst* have many meanings: craving, desire, longing, yearning, eager, emptiness, etc. We hunger and thirst for love, for belonging, to be recognized. We desire peace and justice. We may lust for power and riches. We want and need to be fulfilled, to be happy, to know and experience goodness. We need family, friends and community. We are hungry for the Bread of God's Word and the Bread of Life. Most of all we want to know that God loves and accepts us as we are.

God also is hungry, desiring our love and friendship, here, now, in our earthly life, but also for all eternity. People in need of food are willing to stand in long lines waiting for a little handout that will keep them alive another day. They wait anxiously hoping that the food will not run out before they receive their share. There are no lineups for God's gifts. There is more than enough for everyone, infinite abundance of all that is good. No one will ever need to be spiritually malnourished. It is Advent, the season to remember that God so loved the world that he gave his only Son so that everyone who believes in him may have eternal life.

The Saviour has come. He is risen and among us. He will come again in glory. During his earthly sojourn he always did what God sent him to do, to bring people to faith that leads to eternal life. Sometimes he was disappointed. Jesus laments over the city, "Jerusalem, Jerusalem...How often have I desired to gather your children together as a hen gathers her brood under her wings, but you were unwilling." (LUKE 13:34) What would he say to us today? Are we always willing to allow Jesus do for us what he desires for us? Does he have reason to lament over us?

Let us be more like the Samaritan woman who met Jesus at Jacob's well. He knew all about her sinful life and offered to give her living water. He said, "Those who drink the water that I will give will never be thirsty. The water will become in them a spring of water gushing up to eternal life." Like the woman, let us pray, "Lord, give us this water." And the Holy Spirit will dwell in us so that our spiritual hunger and thirst may always be satisfied. During this time of preparation for celebrating the coming of the Saviour of the world, let us be hungry for the food and drink that leads to eternal life. Let us also concern ourselves with helping to alleviate the hunger of those who face malnutrition and starvation.

Our Father, give us today our daily bread
Remind us to be generous as you are generous
Amen

OUT WITH THE OLD – IN WITH THE NEW

It is New Year's Eve, a time to reflect on the past year with gratitude and look forward to the new with hope. This year has run its course. How has it been for me, for you, for us? What are the good things we will always remember? Are there regrets? Unfinished business? Am I glad it is over so as to get a brand new start tomorrow? Or do I linger with memories and feelings, with some nostalgia for what has been? Remembering is a good activity. Taking time to list all that has been good, all the blessings, all the ups and downs of life this past year, it seems that the only logical response is one of deep gratitude.

There is so much for which to be thankful. There must be at least 365 reasons for gratitude: The gift of life with reasonable good health; the gift of friends and family; our faith community. The gift of God's only Son in Jesus Christ! The freedom to live and celebrate our faith openly in community, the good life we enjoy wherever we live, the gift of winter that straddles the old and the new years, all the seasons, the fresh air, sunshine and clean water, caring health professionals, the ability and freedom to give to charity, to volunteer time and talent. I am particularly grateful for my religious congregation of the School Sisters of Notre Dame, the belonging, support and love.

I could go on, but this is enough to convince me that the year coming to a close has been a very good year. All of you could add much to this list, I am sure. Does all this not give reason to sing God's praises for the goodness of all God's gifts of love?

Out with the old? Not really. All that has been accompanies me into the new. I will leave behind only those habits that are not life giving, the forgiven sins that God has also forgotten, any hurts that I endured from others and also forgive.

What then could be our hopes for the New Year? Hopes can turn into prayers offered up to God for the coming year.

God of all Newness
We hope to be open to whatever daily life offers
We hope to do justice, love kindness and walk humbly
with our loving God (Micah 6:8)
We hope to continue to enjoy the good life we share, to deepen our faith
life in our community that so supports it
We hope to have enough energy and good health
to continue the good we do
We hope and pray for lasting peace in our world
We also hope every person, every family, will be blessed in all the ways
You, oh God, know they need
Amen

THE GIFT OF TIME

Time, what is it? We all have it, twenty-four hours a day, three hundred sixty-five days a year. We are given time during which to live our life. When our time "comes," that is, runs out, we enter into the Eternal Now with our loving God.

On January 1, we were given a new year, an opportunity to begin anew with a clean slate. Most of us have probably made resolutions to somehow become better people and this entails how we use our time. Some of us may even still be faithful in keeping them. Why make resolutions? Deep within our subconscious we desire to make better use of the time given to us. We want to be better people.

Some years ago, I was visiting a dying man. Every time I came into his room I noticed that his brother was always sitting at his side. I learned later that this brother had for years refused to speak with the brother who now lay dying and could no longer speak. The anger and unwillingness to forgive and make up kept these brothers alienated. I wonder what his thoughts were as he watched a brother die. What were his regrets?

We can look at time as so many hours, days or years. Or we can reflect rather on our priorities by which we live these hours, days and years. This morning I received the gift of another new day, another opportunity to begin again. Tonight as I reflect on how I spent my day, it is less important to list all my accomplishments, or lack thereof, than to reflect on how loving I have been. If this were my last day, what would have been important? What would I regret? For what would I be grateful? Jesus says "Keep awake therefore, for you do not know on what day your Lord your Lord is coming." (Mt 24:42)

We have all received the precious gift of time during which to live the precious gift of life. May this New Year be the one to which we can look back and know our

God would say, "Well done, good and faithful servant. You have been a good manifestation of my love for all people."

Loving God, help us to live each moment according to your holy will
Amen

BIRTH AND RESURRECTION

A few years ago, I was going to church during the Christmas season and noticed something very un-Christmas-like in the Nativity scene in front of our church. Behind the crèche on the back panel of the scene an image of the risen Christ was painted. I was touched by how appropriate it was, and each year since I've spent time pondering this mystery.

Without the death and resurrection Jesus' birth would be nothing more than the birth of a beautiful baby. However, Jesus' life did end in redemptive death and resurrection. It is interesting to draw parallels between the birth and death-resurrection of Jesus.

Jesus was born outside the city of Bethlehem; Jesus was crucified outside the city of Jerusalem. Mary wrapped him in swaddling cloths and laid him in a manger within their cave shelter; Nicodemus wrapped his body in linen cloths and laid him in a stranger's rock-hewn tomb. The magi brought gifts fit for a God-King and myrrh, used in burial rites. Myrrh and aloes were spices used to wrap Jesus' body in the linen cloths.

Christmas decorations are put away for another year. Life is going back to normal, to what our church calendar calls "ordinary time." The scripture readings at our Sunday services will take us through the public life of Jesus which concludes with the holy week services commemorating the redemptive work of our Saviour. All this is made possible because God's only Son, Mary's son, was born in a stable outside of the city of Bethlehem. And this event of Jesus' birth is given profound significance by his death and resurrection. That is why the image of the risen Christ in the stable of Jesus' birth is so very appropriate. This gives Christmas a deeper significance than the commemoration of his birth alone. So, back to the outdoor crèche at St. Peter's church with the risen Christ figure on its back wall. I congratulate the designer and artist who created this image of deep mystery.

Thank you, Lord Jesus, for your redemptive coming among us

Amen

ONLY THIS

We have begun a new year. What will this year bring? What does our loving God have in store for us? What is the desire of God's heart? What is the deepest desire of my heart?

We could ask with Israel in Micah 6:6 -7: How shall I come before my God? What great deeds could I perform? What sacrifices? And God answers in verse 8, "Only this, to act justly, to love tenderly and to walk humbly with your God."

It seems a simple enough requirement of our God.

To act justly, in our day to day living, in our interactions with one another is what is asked. It is justice when all share in the goods of this world. It is justice when no person is treated badly, when each one is seen and treated as a child of God loved unconditionally even as I am. When each of us acts justly in all our dealings with one another we contribute greatly to justice in our world.

To love tenderly is to love as God loves. We have just celebrated that "God so loved the world that he gave his only son so that all may have eternal life." (John 3:16) Loving tenderly is to be kind and gentle with one another, nonjudgmental, helpful and generous. It is to love with God's own LOVE which he pours into our hearts. In our world that suffers so much hatred and revenge, every loving act, word and thought on our part increases a loving spirit on Earth.

To walk humbly with our God is to be aware of our being always in God's presence, aware that God's Spirit lives in and among us. This awareness has the effect of seeing others as temples of God, as God's beloved. It is to realize that all is gift from God and to live and work in perpetual gratitude. It is to turn to God in all our needs, to pray for our loved ones, to ask for forgiveness. It is to acknowledge our dependence on God as beloved creatures.

As we put away our Christmas decorations let us continue to pray to the Prince of Peace to transform our hearts into peacemakers in daily life. We may anguish over the state of our world, over women and children being bought and sold as sex slaves or cheap labour. We may experience helplessness and even anger at the violence in wars, in our cities, in homes and neighbourhoods. We may believe that we can do nothing to change these situations. But we can. Every positive thought, word and act has a positive effect on the overall spirit in our world. So each of us can do our small part to make this year a little better. We can also take advantage of opportunities to become more informed about human trafficking, AIDS, child poverty, etc. and perhaps be motivated to act.

Dear God
Help me to live what you ask
to act justly
love tenderly
and walk humbly before you
Amen

PART NINE:
ALL PEOPLE
ARE PRECIOUS

WHO IS GUILTY?

A man is charged with brutally killing and dismembering 26 women involved in the sex trade. In the coming weeks and months we were bombarded with gory details during regular newscasts. What was our response? Were we angry? Disgusted? Sick? Curious? Indifferent? Challenged? Is there a response that we Christians are called to make?

Who was guilty? We know that some man or men committed this horrific crime. Our justice system attempts to determine who and to punish the criminal(s). The judge and jury had an unenviable task to perform and needed our prayer support. I believe our society is also guilty. How could so many women go missing for months and years before real action is taken to find them? Why are women involved in the sex trade singled out for disposal? We know that for every woman working the streets, there are several men also involved in this same sex trade. Why the double standard? Is it like the woman in the gospel caught in the very act of committing adultery...while her partner was not caught? (JOHN 8:3-4)

All the murdered women were someone's daughter, sister, and even mother. Each got lost in drugs and prostitution at an early age. They needed to be rescued and healed, not murdered as throw away trash. Every woman thus treated diminishes all women – and men. Our society is in dire need of conversion.

How can each of us help? We all have women in our families and among our friends. Each of us can most likely improve the respect and honour we give them. Young boys need to be taught and shown that girls are just as important and precious and valuable as boys. The example of fathers and male teachers and coaches is very important. And girls need to be assured of this through word and action. Our society is largely patriarchal which makes it easy to act as though males are greater than females. Yet when God created human beings we were all, male and female, made in the image and likeness of God. "So God created humankind in his image, in the image of God he created them; Male and female he created them." (GENESIS 1:27)

When reading the gospels we notice how Jesus treated women differently from the accepted patriarchal way. What did he do when the woman caught in adultery was brought to him? He treated her with gentleness and forgiveness, unlike the Scribes and Pharisees who would have stoned her. The whole story is in JOHN 8: 1-11.

We represent God and are gifted with the power of the Holy Spirit. Let us treasure each person in our life, and speak against the mistreatment of others, in our neighbourhood, our country, our world, and pray for the end of the heinous crime of human trafficking. Believe that every loving thought, word and action of ours raises the overall spirit in our world.

Creator and loving God
Help us to be good representatives of your loving concern for all
Amen

GOD'S REPRESENTATIVES

Pentecost Sunday is the day we celebrate that the Spirit of God is within and among us. With the gathered disciples we have received the outpouring of the Holy Spirit. As a Christian people we have the wisdom, the understanding and courage to make good and caring decisions. Representing God gives us privileges and responsibilities.

All the resources of our Earth are available to us and we hear and read daily of our need to take better care if we want our children and grandchildren to have a healthier environment. There is one resource also belonging to God that is getting too little attention, namely, people. The women and children who are bought and sold like commodities cry out to our God for help.

Some of the causes of trafficking include:

• Profitability. It is a $9 billion a year industry. Unlike drugs or arms, people can be sold many times.

• Growing deprivation and marginalization of the poor. Victims are promised good and respectable jobs. Sometimes parents sell their children on a promise that they will receive education and a better life. Their situations are so desperate that they believe the fraudulent stories.

• Insufficient penalties against traffickers.

• According to the UN a major factor that has allowed the growth of sexual trafficking is "Governments and human rights organizations alike have simply judged the woman guilty of prostitution and minimized the trafficker's role."

Globally, it is estimated that between 700,000 and 2 million people each year fall victim to human trafficking. Does this have anything to do with us? Are our children not susceptible to cyberspace seduction?

The information I share comes from the Internet, the *Prairie Messenger* and from my community of the School Sisters of Notre Dame. Trafficking of human persons for the sex trade or slave labour is a very serious form of slavery today. God cares for all the people he created, sees all of us as very good. How is it that human life and some persons are so expendable? What can our response be?

We represent God and are gifted with the power of the Holy Spirit. Let us treasure each person in our life, speak against the mistreatment of others in our neighborhood, our country, our world and pray for the end of this heinous crime of human trafficking, believing that every loving thought, word and action of our raises the overall spirit in our world.

Prayer for an End to Trafficking

O God, our words cannot express
what our minds can barely comprehend
and our hearts feel
when we hear of women and children deceived
and transported to unknown places

for purposes of sexual exploitation and abuse
because of human greed and profit
at this time in our world

Our hearts are saddened and our spirits angry
that their dignity and rights
are being transgressed through threats,
deception and force

We cry out against the degrading practice of trafficking
and pray for it to end
Strengthen the fragile-spirited and broken-hearted
Make real your promises to fill these victims
with a love that is tender and good
and send the exploiters away empty-handed
Give us wisdom and courage
to stand in solidarity with them
that together we will find ways
to the freedom that is your gift to all of us
We make our prayer through Jesus Christ
who loves all unconditionally

Amen

A Special Note on Human Trafficking

Human trafficking is a growing lucrative business with woman and children being the biggest commodity. The School Sisters of Notre Dame have formed a very active Stop Human Trafficking Committee and the following pages have been submitted by Sister Theresa Nagle. They include the kind of work the committee does and some heartrending stories of real trafficked people.

August 27, 2013

Our Stop Human Trafficking Committee began in 2004 and started doing educational presentations to different groups in the Hamilton, Halton and Kitchener-Waterloo areas and beyond. Why did we start and continue this?

We believe that God created everyone to have dignity and worth and Jesus always showed that.

This is the 21st century slave trade and is a multibillion-dollar business. Victims (women and children) are seen as *nobodies* and are treated as such. They are showing profit over people (life). Human trafficking is second among the three highest criminal activities (drugs and guns are the highest) but it is the least known.

A few years after we began, our committee began purchasing purple roses for ourselves and to sell them at our presentations. They were created by the Gabriela for the Purple Rose Campaign around 1999 to stop human trafficking of Filipino women and children. This became an international movement. Most of our committee members wear the pin. It is attractive and a conversation piece.

Why a purple rose? Roses, by nature, were never purple. Purple roses were bred, made exotic by human will. The purple rose exists not for its own evolutionary purposes but for the pleasure and profit of others. Women and children victims of trafficking are no different from the purple rose. They are reduced to becoming mere objects of pleasure and sources of profit. Forced by poverty, commodified and enslaved by globalization, women and children have become Purple Roses.

by Theresa Nagel, SSND

Recent Canadian Stories

Emily's Story

I lost my mother to HIV/AIDS when I was only 14 years old. I had to drop out of school to take care of my younger brother and sister. I was always really worried about money and our future.

One of my uncles told me that he had a friend who was willing to help our family. My uncle's friend told me that he had special connections in Canada. I believed him. The "friend" promised me a job as a nanny that would last a year, and offered to pay for my plane ticket up front. He told me that I would make enough money to support my family back home as well as have some savings for future education.

I did not want to leave my family, but felt the risk was worth it because it was only for one year and I had limited options for myself and family at home.

Upon arrival in Canada, I discovered that the "family" I was supposed to live with did not exist. I had to pay off my plane ticket by working. Then, to my horror, I discovered this work meant having sex with me. I was deeply mortified, and found myself crying throughout the night. I was given a new name, and my passport was taken.

I often thought about escaping, yet I was afraid of the police and being thrown in jail.

Jasmine's Story

Hi, my name is Jasmine and I was a sex slave. I did not start out that way and if you had told me when I was 18 that my life would have taken that direction I would have said *no way!* I was born and raised in North Bay, Ontario, in a Christian home and came to the University of Western Ontario to study pre-med, as I had wanted to be a doctor. When I arrived, I was swept away by the freedom I suddenly had and I wanted to and did use my tuition money to shop, shop, shop for all the lovely things I wanted but never really had while living at home. At this point I found myself running out of money, since I couldn't live on campus anymore. I also had to buy specific food as I had Crohns' Disease, and so I took a job as a waitress at a bar in London to earn money for tuition and shopping. But soon I discovered that I did not have enough money and that is when I met my boyfriend.

I began selling shots while waitressing to earn even more money. I had bills to pay—condo fees and money required for shopping. It was at this time the bar was being renovated and the girls had to go elsewhere and so I left school and became a dancer. Still I did not have enough money and so I began stripping to earn more. I would have died if my parents had known what I was doing, but I figured that no one back home would ever find out. The more I shopped, the more I got sucked into the material world, and the more I needed to strip for more money. Suddenly, I found myself not going to school, not studying and still with bills to pay. I was hoping that I would be able to get out of debt and then go back to school.

I decided to move to Toronto, where I met a very handsome young man who treated me like a queen, paying for everything, buying me everything I wanted, and even making me go back to school. I was thrilled and couldn't believe my good luck to have someone who cared so much and could provide so much. He even provided me with an apartment. But then, he started moving girls into the apartment with me and asked me to look after them. I thought this would be okay, until one day I realized that he was a pimp and these girls were his prostitutes and they had to hand over to him all the money that they were earning.

At this point, I freaked out and tried to escape and even phone my mom to help me but my Mom didn't even know where to begin to help me. I had a week to move out of the apartment, which I successfully did. At this point in time, I thought I had escaped and all was well for me. Then one day, as I came home to my new condo, there he was, waiting outside my condo door. He punched and choked me, took my cell, beat me up and never let me out of his sight, forcing me to get his name tattooed on my body. And so, the spiral began again.

He became my pimp. He kept everything I earned and he owned everything I had. I was beaten every two or three days and forced to have sex or perform sexual acts with men I didn't even know. For two and a half years I lived this hell and I prayed to God every day for death, as I hated what was happening to me and that was the only way I could see to end it.

I knew this lifestyle was wrong, but I trusted no one and did not talk to anyone about it, even my family. Every time we spoke, I told them all was fine, but of course, it was not – I was a prostitute and so ashamed and I thought that God couldn't love me anymore. I honestly thought I loved this man, so brainwashed was I, and then I discovered that I was pregnant. My boyfriend proposed to me in Cuba, and subsequently took away my passport. I accepted because I had to protect my baby and this was the only way I knew how. Eventually I confided in my brother and at eight weeks pregnant, I told my boyfriend that I was leaving, but he broke into the house and forced me to be with him, saying he would take care of me. He went after my brother, who is only 5'7" and my boyfriend/pimp is 6'3." My bother went to the York Regional Police where he was told that the victim must speak up herself or there should be a witness to these acts. Of course, there was no witness and I was brainwashed and would not speak up against my pimp, because I believed that I loved him.

Eventually, I became homeless because my "boyfriend" would no longer pay for anything and so I had to work right after the birth of my daughter in order to support her and myself. I did not want to return to the sex trade industry and so, gathering all the strength I could find, I went back to church, the Maple Community. I once again quit school and did what I could to get by, without prostituting myself. And all this time, I prayed to God to open the right doors for me, please. All along, my bother kept emailing me and finally I opened up to a youth worker who told me that I needed to help myself before I could help others.

This I believed to be God speaking to me and helping me. I tried getting help from Canada Fights Human Trafficking but that did not work so I was passed off to a group called Sex Trade 101, who helped me tremendously, by getting me an Ontario Works permit, an apartment and support throughout the trial. My "boyfriend"/pimp was sentenced to two years for assault, sexual assault and living off the avails of prostitution.

I am now free of my pimp and am a speaker for Sex Trade 101 and have two children and a wonderful supportive fiancé. I believe this turned out this way for me because I put my faith in God and asked Him to help me out of this horrible mess, and He did...I just wasn't listening and when I did, then life changed for me.

Thank you for your support for me and for other trafficked victims.

Dear God, forgive us, the people you made in your own image and likeness, for the ways we abuse one another for our own gain. Help us love deeply and pray that those who buy and sell women and children will be touched by your divine grace. Be with the victims and send helping healing people into their lives

Amen

THE INSIGNIFICANT HAS POWER

The first snowfall of the season always surprises us even though we also expect it any time after Halloween. There is something so wonderfully beautiful about snow. Each snowflake is unique in its geometric design, truly a thing of beauty to be admired. But snowflakes never stay isolated and alone. They are joined together to provide the stuff for making snowmen and to get the ski slopes ready for the season. Despite the cold and the inconvenience of shovelling and scraping the car free of the white stuff, I appreciate the beauty of snow. On the other hand, piles of snow partnered with wind can close roads, break trees and ground planes. Shovelling and plowing become backbreaking and wearisome tasks.

All this gives food for reflection on the power of the seemingly insignificant. Like the snowflake, a smile, a greeting, a word of encouragement can make the day for the recipients. I never know how far my smile, my greeting my words of affirmation travel. They get 'paid forward' in ways I will never know. The opposite is also true. My negative words, my gossip, my judgments, also get paid forward in ways I will never know.

There is a story about a woman who was known as the town gossip. In her efforts to overcome this bad habit she confessed to her pastor. For penance he gave her a bag of feathers to go and empty into the wind. Then she was to return with the empty bag. She was pleased to have fulfilled this penance knowing that the wind had carried her gossip away. Was she in for a surprise! "Now go out and gather all those feathers if you can." Of course that was impossible. So it is with gossip or any other negativity we spread. It takes on a life of its own and it is impossible to take it back.

There is another story in JOHN 4. A Samaritan woman had a lengthy conversation with Jesus at Jacob's well. Having discovered that Jesus was the Messiah, she ran back to her village proclaiming, "Come and see a man who told me everything I have ever done! Can he be the Messiah?" Her joy and enthusiasm brought the villagers to accept Jesus into their midst.

Lord Jesus, help us to be nonjudgmental with our friends and neighbors,
truthful and contrite about ourselves and leave all the judging to your
loving heart
Amen

CONCLUSION

When I began writing articles for our local paper, I never dreamed that they could be published in a book. But with encouragement from several people, here it is – a book! As I re-read articles to edit and improve it became apparent that I have basically one message: God loves us, each one of us, unconditionally!

I learned this simple yet profound truth a long time ago. When I was three or four years old, I was looking at a picture of the Good Shepherd. He held a lamb in his arms while the adult sheep stood around his feet. My mom told me that Jesus loves and cares for me like that little lamb. She then tucked me into bed and I felt totally loved, by Jesus and my mom.

In all my life I never unlearned this truth. I have always believed and experienced God's unconditional love. Even when I was experiencing the hard things in life and relationships, I always knew God loves me unconditionally and always. I pray that my humble reflections will help others grow in their trust and acceptance of God's unconditional love for them.

God is love and that is what God does: Love! "See what love the Father has given us that we should be called children of God; and that is what we are...God is love, and those who abide in love abide in God, and God abides in them." (1 JOHN 3:1, 17)

All praise and thanks to our God for loving us!

Valentia Leibel

ABOUT THE AUTHOR

Sister Valentia Leibel joined the School Sisters of Notre Dame when she was just 17. She chose them, she says, because "they were an international congregation and I wanted to be in a position where I could teach the world about God's love." She first focused her attention on academic pursuits. After completing high school and teachers' college in Ontario, she taught mostly primary grades for about 10 years in Ontario and Edmonton, Alberta. During this time, she earned a Bachelor of Arts degree from the University of Alberta in Edmonton.

After Vatican II, the Edmonton Catholic Schools required consultants of religious education.

She studied at the Divine Word Centre in London, Ontario and St. Paul's University in Ottawa, Ontario and graduated with a Master's Degree in Religious Education.

She served as Religious Education Consultant for eight years in the Edmonton (Alberta) Separate Schools and Halton County (Ontario) Separate Schools. Working in the parish ministry in Burlington (Ontario) and in the rural communities of Luseland and Tramping Lake in Saskatchewan gave her valuable insights into the lives of families and the struggles they faced.

For six years, she served as Religious Educator in the Archdiocese of Regina, Saskatchewan.

During this time her ministry consisted mainly in training parents and grandparents to teach religion to the children in their rural parishes. Her years in the Keewatin-le-Pas Archdiocese enriched her experiences in working with Aboriginal communities. This required many modes of travel, broadening her understanding of the vast differences of people in Canada and the challenge to be unified in faith.

Sister Val currently lives in Unity, Saskatchewan. Adapted from columns written over several years in area community and religious publications, *Heart of God* is her first book.

SCHOOL SISTERS OF NOTRE DAME (SSND)

The School Sister of Notre Dame (SSND). Who are we? We are an international Congregation of Apostolic Women Religious. We express our mission through ministry directed toward education. For us education means enabling people to become the persons God created them to be. We educate with the conviction that the world can be changed through the transformation of persons.

We were founded in Germany by Blessed Theresa of Jesus Gerhardinger in 1833. She struggled against many odds to remain a united international community. Even in her lifetime her sisters were sent to the USA, Canada, England and several European countries. And so today we are united internationally, serving in 34 countries. Daily we struggle to live this unity together in a divided world.

Approximately 1800 SSNDs serve in 33 states in the USA. In Canada we are in five provinces from Ontario to British Columbia and in the north West Territories. Canadian sisters also serve in England, Africa, Paraguay, Puerto Rico and Italy.

We go forth daily in the spirit of Blessed Theresa, remembering her words: "Poor and abandoned, we began this work of God in supernatural faith and confidence. Let us continue to serve the Triune God all our lives with joy, to obey him, to love him above all."

Blessed Mother Theresa, pray for all School Sisters of Notre Dame, your sisters, and continue to inspire us in our vocation.

May 1980 Paula 1st. Communion